Beneath

Our

Numbers

Beneath Our Numbers

A Collaborative Memoir From Inside Mass Incarceration

Jerrod Buford

Charles Butcher

Carter Cooper

Ashleigh Dye

Tony Enis

Ricardo Ferrell

Chiron Francis

Dushaan Gillum

John Green

John Johnson

Timothy Johnson

Delaine Jones

Joshua Kenyon

Robert Linton

Geoff Martin

Charles Mamou, Jr.

Tevin Nero

Resolute

Terry Robinson

Louis Singleton, Jr.

Phillip Vance Smith, II

George Wilkerson

Jarod Wesenberg

Introduction

The perspective that compassion and rehabilitation for those who live in prison is an attack on victims of crime oversimplifies a complex issue. The reflections included in this book, written in prison, are intended to inspire conversations. Including these voices in the pursuit of justice reform and while weighing retribution against rehabilitation, increases the productivity of those conversations.

Walk In Those Shoes (WITS) shares the combined history of a family of writers living in prisons across the United States. These words are not intended to excuse, but rather to inform and broaden the dialogue. The writing also lends insight into the impact of various forms of trauma on human development and what rehabilitation sometimes looks like.

Innocence is also reflected here. Any conversation, book, program, podcast or interview that addresses the criminal justice system and neglects to include the innocent is incomplete. The system victimized some of these writers, who are innocent of the crimes they are serving time for. They, all too often, get overlooked.

WITS is a 501(c)(3) founded to encourage reading and writing in prison while raising awareness. The writers represented here are a diverse bunch, yet their lives share similarities. They are bound by a love of writing and shared circumstances, but varied by individual character, views, personalities and experiences.

While compiling this collection, I received a letter from a WITS writer. His concerns and reflection speak to why WITS exists. He wrote, *"I max my sentence out in about nine months. I've had nearly a decade in complete isolation, a myriad of health and mental health problems and will be going to Erie, Pennsylvania to be homeless, broke and confused as to what the hell they expect to happen. I don't know what aspect of these twelve years constitutes 'rehabilitation', but I'm afraid that I'm a tragedy waiting to happen. Still, I'm glad I've found poetry toward the end of my incarceration because it not only gave me a cathartic outlet, but it also enabled me to preserve a piece of myself in poem."*

Some of these writers are serving life sentences. Some are on death row. Some are innocent. Many have served decades. Some were youthful offenders. These are their stories, overlapping at times, and often eerily similar.

I Write

by Tony Enis

I write to escape,
To hide deep within
Where I can be alone
With my hidden thoughts
And secret hopes.
That secret place
Is mine alone,
I can hide my torment,
Anguish and despair,
Where it need not be on display
For the world to see.

I write to bury my pain,
To cast it aside with pen and paper.
With the stroke of a pen,
I create my own illusion
Of joy and happiness.
But the illusion is a lie,
And like all lies,
It cannot stand up to the light of day.
I write the words my mouth cannot speak,
The words that lay trapped
In the deepest depths of this well
That is my heart.
I cannot give voice to those words,
For then they would become
A part of my reality
And no longer could I seek sanctuary
In the illusion,
In the lie that cannot stand up to the light of day.
I write to stay alive inside,
To keep from dying
A little more with each passing day,
To keep love at bay as she nips at my heart.
Because for me, to love is to die,

Not physically, but inside,
A little more each day.
So, write I must
As love kicks and pounds
At the door of my heart.
That is why I write...

Our Roots Run Deep

There are well-known risk factors associated with incarceration, among them adverse childhood experiences, trauma, poverty, race and substance abuse.

Goodbye Never

by Terry Robinson

I'll never forget that summer day in '78 when my childhood innocence was shattered. I was four, the sun was out, and my only interest was in candy and fun. We lived in Mary Ellis trailer park, a scant neighborhood on the lower eastside of town. Everyone was treated like family in Mary Ellis. Even the insurance guy and the mailman were often shown hospitality. It was a fine community to grow up in – until that day when everything changed.

I was playing in the yard with my cousin, Teeka, when my urge for sweets kicked in. My mom was at my Aunt Helen's trailer, a few lots down, while another aunt of mine babysat us. Teeka was four also and convincing her to sneak away was never difficult. Our capers were usually performed as a duo.

We started out for Ms. Rolee's, a nearby elderly woman who sold penny candy and cookies to the neighborhood kids. Though Ms. Rolee wasn't home, my sugar cravings went undeterred. Try-Me-Foods was a bodega located across the roadway that supplied people in the neighborhood with second-rate groceries on credit. Even though I was forbidden by my mom from crossing the busy street while unsupervised, I still set my sights there. Teeka and I scampered over to Try-Me-Foods, traded our coins for tarts and darted back. Once safely across, we considered the candy evidence and tore into the wrappers with our teeth.

Suddenly, a loud pop rang out and reverberated throughout Mary Ellis. Startled by the unexpectedness of the sound, our steps came to a halt. Teeka's sparkly hazel eyes dimmed with fright as she clutched my hand tight. I'd heard a car backfire before, which sounded similar. I was about to explain the noise to Teeka when a series of rapid pops bellowed out. That was no mechanical hiccup.

I took off running with Teeka in tow as she did her best to keep up. Such a volatile sequence gave a clear indication of danger and left me concerned for my mom. Only when we arrived at Aunt Helen's trailer did Teeka and I break speed. That's when I saw Uncle Jimmy, Helen's estranged husband, behind the wheel of his blue Chevy Nova. Whirling tires spat dust and gravel as he backed the manic machine into the street and barely avoided smashing a parked car. His chestnut skin glistened with perspiration, his frantic face hardened. As Uncle Jimmy scoured for an escape, I thought to wave goodbye.

Just as quickly, I was reminded of the concern for my mother, and I pushed Uncle Jimmy's hazardous departure aside. I turned to the trailer. On busted hinges, the door hung ajar while the sounds of faint soul music and whimpers drifted from within. I climbed the steps, stretched out my hand and opened the door wider.

Lying on his back, head first, was Curtis, a family friend who courted Aunt Helen. A dapper man with tinted shades and neatly trimmed afro, I was accustomed to seeing Curtis often. He would toss me high above his head, catch me in his arms, then say that I was his main man. I liked Curtis, particularly because I was always tallest when in his arms.

But now Curtis wasn't standing, all smiles and ready to hoist me in the air. His afro was pushed aside in a disheveled heap while a pool of crimson liquid gathered beneath him. His shades were crooked in a way that revealed his closed eyes. Something was terribly wrong with Curtis, but I couldn't decide what.

I was even more perplexed by Aunt Helen, who lay slumped at Curtis' feet. Her body was sprawled across his, like a fallen shield at battle's end. On her forehead was a cruel mark that oozed red with a distant glare in her eyes that bore through me. "Aunt Helen. Aunt Helen, get up," I pleaded, though I knew she couldn't hear me. She and Curtis had transcended beyond the ways of sound.

I would never look at life or death the same after that day. Part of me would stand on those steps for eternity, haunted by the gruesome scene before me. As blood spewed from their tangled bodies, my childhood innocence seeped away. I'd peeped through the doorway of a domestic dispute and saw the wrath of love turned deadly. I'd witnessed the removal of three influential people in my life, whose absence carved an emotional chasm. The facade of life crumbled under the weight of Uncle Jimmy's mercilessness, and yet the thing that stands out most is that I never got to tell him goodbye.

Kindred

by Resolute

The summer between second and third grade was a dark period in my young life. It was also the summer I met an angel.

I've always believed I was a miracle of birth, an unexplainable phenomenon – that is, if my mother wasn't pulling my leg about everything. I soon began to realize my being born dead was merely a footnote in a life plagued by misery before it even began. Yet at the age of seven, I thought my life was normal, the same as everyone else's. Then everything changed. First came the car accident. My father grabbed my little brother and ran, never looking back, leaving me and my unconscious mother. I wondered if he gave us a second thought as I watched his back going down the street.

Not long after that I got into a mysterious fight with two brothers – who were my best friends. I later found out my father paid my friends to jump me.

Like an unstoppable tsunami, those events damaged my soul. The reality I thought I knew was forever shattered. *I was stripped of my illusions.* I could trust no one, not even my own parents.

Then I met an angel, a force of nature. My father drank and gambled a lot, and he often took me to strangers' homes where I would find myself sitting on unfamiliar porches for hours. Wary. Until other kids would try to make me leave. I had so many fights, I lost count. I sometimes found myself wondering if I was what the adults were really gambling on. That's why I was expecting trouble when the door to the upstairs apartment opened. The Knox family lived there. That summer Neal Knox, who was older than me, became my nemesis.

I was surprised when the person who exited wasn't Neal or his mother but a girl my age. Her hazel eyes drank in the environment, and she stared at me as if she knew my thoughts. "Do you want some candy?" Without waiting for my reply, she sat down and divided the bag.

Then she smiled, revealing a deep set of dimples, before saying absentmindedly, "Oh, my name is Tiffany."

As we talked, I learned she and her mother were visiting. Neal was her cousin. We soon decided to go play with the other kids from the area. Being kids, someone eventually dared everybody to go into an abandoned house down the street. Everyone believed the place was haunted. I had to go. I wanted to prove I wasn't afraid. So what the house was a condemned, burned out husk. So what we'd all get into big trouble if we got caught. So what if everybody believed the house was haunted. I needed to do it!

We made it to the second floor. How, I don't know, because all of us were afraid. We were bunched together like sheep surrounded by hungry wolves. Then someone screamed they'd seen a ghost. Neal and many others ran. I ran too, only my feet carried me further into the empty, soot-covered room in search of the ghost. I noticed immediately I wasn't alone. Without doubt or hesitation Tiffany had come with me. From that moment onward, we were inseparable.

We did everything together. We played tag. We raced. We tumbled. We even climbed trees till our hands hurt. The field house at the park and our neighborhood community center offered lots of programs and we joined. Swimming. Gymnastics. Basketball. Little league baseball. After I turned eight, we began martial arts classes. Tiffany continuously supported and practiced with me. Her belief in me enabled me to believe in myself.

When the new school year began, Tiffany was in my class. The school we went to was only a block and a half from where I lived, but I'd walk three blocks in the wrong direction just to walk with Tiffany.

One day during our lunch break, Tiffany and I were racing the half block to the neighborhood store. We ran to the crossing guard to get to the store before it got crowded. I got there first. That had begun to happen a lot.

I was standing and looking to see how long we'd have to wait when a blur suddenly passed me. I watched as a car hit whoever had been standing there. I saw their body as it went under the car and was in shock being so close to something like that. I couldn't move, and I watched the small, mangled body as it got twisted around the tire's axle. People appeared from everywhere trying to save whoever was hit. The drunk driver tried to drive away but the crowd pulled her out through the car's window.

A small unmoving body was pulled from under the car. In my catatonic state I could barely breathe, much less think clearly. As I watched, they pulled Tiffany's body out. But how? She was supposed to be standing next to me...

I've mourned Tiffany my entire life. In the eight months and thirteen days I knew her, she showed me with her every action how much she believed in me every day. She believed in me before I believed in myself. I carry her memory with me always. Whenever I find myself at my lowest, Tiffany reminds me to believe in myself. I know she would.

The Inheritance
by Phillip Vance Smith, II

the inheritance
my father told me a story once
it was only one of a few... you see
he was a stranger
a deadbeat i barely knew... anyway
he ran me out the front door
into a ghetto summer outside
his little duplex was a waste of space
on chicago's black southside
he pointed up forest avenue
like a man waving a gun
squinting at some invisible foe
escaping on the run
"your grandpa stood right here," he said

in a wife beater stained with paint
he shouted to that midnight burglar
"I may be drunk, but I sho' shoot straight"
he laughed and slapped my back
he doubled over to wheeze
then he stood up clutching his belly
reminiscing his fond memory
the ghetto sun faded
to a dark, blackish hue
my grandpa died a dirty drunk
and so will the father i barely knew
the inheritance

How To Drown

by Delaine Jones

I can't swim. I can't even float. It's not very dignified for a former athlete, but I paddle like a dog, and I'm ashamed to admit my little sister taught herself to swim before I ever knew what dog paddling was.

Some would say that learning to swim is about overcoming large fears. Others would say it's about overcoming the fear of death and gaining confidence in self. To not learn to swim efficiently

speaks of some form of cowardice, a lack of heart –
something that can't be taught. The ability is held
in such high regard that fathers throw their
frightened children into the deep, forcing them to
literally 'sink or swim'.

I was eight years old when I left the three-foot end
of the pool to get in line to dive off the high dive
and into the twelve-foot end. I knew I couldn't
swim, and I was likely to die. I simply did not care
to let this chance pass me by. Some would claim
I'd been thrown into the deep end long before that
moment.

My heart threatened to break a rib with its
hammering, but I'd been my little sister's protector
and her go-to, and whenever she called my name,
I'd never failed to answer the bell. I could not
allow her to continue to see me fail, to see me in
fear. So, I got in line. I braved the line not only to
confront my fear of death, but my fear of seeing
disappointment in my lil sister's eyes. Truth be
told, there were few things in life I feared more.
Her love and adoration were, in my mind, forever

bound to my ability to protect her, to lead the way, to provide something that neither of us had. Self-worth maybe? Identity?

It all began before that day at the pool. We lived in Compton, California, on Primrose Street. I was still young, it was before I'd started school, before crack and the justice system ravaged my family, but after my mom was murdered. My "G"-mom was simply trying to do right by her daughter's children, keeping us together, safe and fed while trying to keep herself together mentally and emotionally. She was trying to find a way to hold on to her God's hand while her own heart and hands were overflowing with pain.

My granny must have been watching from the shadow of the screen door when my sister and I were fighting in the backyard over a toy. To win, I pushed her down, and she began to cry. In a flash, the door banged open, and my grandmother had me in her clutches. She lit into me in a real way, and through my tears, she took my cheeks in her hand and pointed to the little girl on the ground.

"That is *your* sister, not some stranger on the street, but *your sister*! You are the *only* big brother she has! Don't you *ever* hurt her, and you better not let anyone else ever hurt her!! Do you hear me?!"

Where I come from there's a phrase for learning to face the very real dangers of life outside the protection of your home. We refer to facing death and learning to survive in the deep end as 'stepping off the porch'. This was my splash! moment.

I was in middle school when I stabbed a middle-schooler for pushing my lil sister down and taking her money as she waited in the candy store line for me. I'd come home with my sister in hand and a black eye that was talking to me. I'd confronted the kid and he took a swing — my first fight ever. He parked me on my butt like he was taking a driver's test. My black eye elicited a warning from my granny. She'd better not hear from that school about me fighting, she'd sent me to school to learn, not to fight. No one cared to ask why I had a black eye. Why should they? This was my little sister, not theirs, so it was up to me to deal with it, right?

When my uncles and grandmother found out what happened from my sister and my attempt to wash my bloody school clothes with some Tide, a hairbrush and the water hose, they all called me crazy. Angry. 'Touched'. All but my grandmother. She never condemned me over what I'd done, nor did she admonish me over the situation. She merely looked at me with a new tilt of curiosity to her head, like she was seeing me for the first time.

I bounced twice from the high dive and did a triple tuck back flip (my grade school had a gymnastics team). I hit the water head first with my arms extended to break the surface, body like an arrow. Best dive of the day! Then I sank right to the bottom, twelve feet of water!

Panic? Never that. I could see the ladder on the other side of the pool. I'd just 'walk' over to it and climb out. I pushed off to get a few sips of air into taxed lungs, only to start panting like a dog. A few sips wouldn't do! Sputtering and choking and thrashing, I sank again. I fought the older kid who came from behind to save me, thinking it was an attack. I sank yet again! I passed out in the pool. My lil sis watched me die trying to lead the way – to continue to be her hero. They dragged my lifeless body from the pool and revived me.

Welcome to my deep end.

I once had to face down a kid who had his heart set on chopping me with a machete over my sister. Once brained a grown man with a brick who tried to rape her. I'm otherwise a non-confrontational person, but when it comes to my mother's only daughter? I would hurt you. Bad.

What I didn't know was that there were threats in our own home. Family members came to live with us, having fallen on tough times financially. I was only a kid, mom was dead – murdered – and neither of our fathers were worth the ink it would cost to write their names. I never knew the love and trust garnered from helping with homework could lead to the ripping of a soul or that the resulting screams are seldom heard because those who cause them are likely the same who stand at the gates in defense.

When she became pregnant at fifteen due to this molestation, I was in chains already, after being on the row for months. My lil sis was alone. She came to see me – alone. Her belly large, her eyes pregnant with fear and secret pain. We held each other and wept, just as we had in the backyard in Compton, California, on Primrose Street. We both drowned that day. Who knows, maybe if I had learned to swim, things could have been different. Maybe some cries can only be heard under water, when you are out of breath – in the deep end.

BOOM

by Delaine Jones

My grandmother had a stroke while sitting on the sofa reading the newspaper. She had mis-read an article about the escape of my crime partner. In the article, my name was used to explain our high-profile case. Thinking I had escaped too, she had a stroke. In her mind and experience, black men in conflict with white authority meant my death/murder. $1 + 1 = 2$. Facts! She never spoke again.

Most believe change is like travel, taking you just as long to return from that wrong spot in life as it took you to get there. *They're wrong.* Change is delivered within the heart of an explosion! There's a *BOOM!* of action. It's how mothers lift cars off their children, how addicts stiff arm drugs and how people find themselves back in school after the age of forty in pursuit of a degree. It's a *BOOM!* - not a slow process.

I was eleven years old the first time I was chosen to play on the junior neighborhood basketball team. Twelve to fifteen lowriders of people from four or five different Blood gangs and Piru hoods would gather in this or that park. It wasn't just a tournament, it was part car show, part cookout, part fashion show. People would show up in their bright 'hood colors, sporting both new and old R.I.P. shirts and hats. The girls and women wore cut off shorts, lip gloss shining, hair freshly pressed, permed, and curled, with edges laid down like a senator before a lobbyist. Boys and men with fresh cuts and cornrows, ice-white t-shirts and matching kicks that lived in a box most of the year.

Black and brown faces flashed brilliantly at me, setting complexions and spirits ablaze, sparkles of pride and joy flashing in the eyes of everyone I met. It was like an African village in my mind, and we were all family. All love. All good. All 'hood. Nothing is ever 'one thing' to all people in life.

After the weekend long tournament, we were heading back home with my Uncle James and his wife Lisa. Myself and two of my homeboy teammates were in the backseat of Unc's '72 Impala lowrider. Carl was bragging about his skills in a tournament we'd lost, no less. Kilo was asleep in the corner.

When the red and blue lights filled our car, it froze my heart as I recalled images I'd seen of police beatings, battering rams, black men being choked out, half-clad black women being dragged from beds into streets, babies torn from arms and hearing screams that are colored red and blue to this day.

I elbowed Kilo awake as my uncle swore in frustration and rage at what he knew was to come.

"Fuck!" he banged the wheel, "Boys, put your hands on the roof, and don't move until they get you out of the car, *and don't say shit!*" Fear led to anger, trying to get us home alive.

Aunty Lisa stuffed two grams of marijuana in her mouth, handing some butts to Unc, both placing their hands on the dash as the second squad car pulled up. The officers spilled out to help circle our car, their hands on their guns, angry eyes and stone set faces. What did they see in our eyes?

One approached the window, and Unc asked why he was stopped, demanding to know. They pulled us out, and we were hand-cuffed, facedown on the sidewalk, still warm from the setting sun. "We smell marijuana. Tear it up!"

"If you're going to search us, call a female to search my wife!" my uncle demanded. He'd been talking the entire time, drawing their attention.

A cop dropped a knee on his head, splitting it open on the concrete, growling, "Shut the fuck up, bitch! I'm sick of your fuckin' mouth!"

Aunt Lisa cried out. I looked back at the other kids, turning away from Carl's tears so he wouldn't see my own. Kilo's eyes were trying to eat up his face, shared fear bonding us for life.

They kept searching us and tearing up the car, but when they got to Aunty Lisa, Unc lost it. The cop on his head pulled his gun and let off a shot into the grass next to my uncle James' head. That's when Lisa lost it, Unc bucked, and the beating began, Josh Gibson-like swings that sent blood sailing through the night air like rubies dancing under the red and blue lights.

My uncle would need 87 stitches to close up his body and head. He'd lose the hearing in his left ear, the sight in his left eye and his motor skills would be forever impaired. He'd also lose his mind and memory in part. He'll forever need care, requiring someone to help his confusion and explain the situation to him daily.

I was numb and frozen until the boom of the gun, until Unc's life pooled on the sidewalk, until I saw one of his braids soaked in that life laying in the dirt.

Aunty Lisa was the only one to notice I was having serious issues, in need of help. "We've got to fight back!" she cried as she hugged me tight, her tears baptizing me into a new light, a new attitude, my value – duty or honor maybe?

"We've got to fight back, because they're never goin' to stop swingin' on us," she cried, trying to set my young, battered mind and spirit for the war she knew would be my life. A war she was sure I'd already lost. It was in the way she held me.

To flip it, it didn't take more than a fraction of a second for me to pull that trigger and change the world for countless others, people I'll never meet. They feel that fraction of a second every day.

Is there a 'boom' when the change is positive? Or is it drowned out in the echoing reverb of so much negativity? Does it count if it goes unheard? And if not heard or recognized, did it happen at all?

Time is the only measuring rod, and change is the only thing to be measured. It should be forever flowing, constantly cutting into the landscape of a life in ways both unforeseen and unpredictable, forcing us to feel everything or hide from it. To lie.

My Aunt Lisa would be found naked on the side of the road in some bushes in the state of Arkansas. I can only pray she knows that I'm still fighting back, because she was right – they'll never stop swinging. I've changed. *Boom!*

Twelve

by Jarod Wesenberg

The first time I put my lips to a crack pipe...

Whoever would've thought I'd indulge in that life?

Mover Man Chris showed me how to smoke it,

Inhale. Inhale. Now, hold it!

I held it... until I had to release it.

Cloud 9, no longer a cliché,

For I had reached it.

I learned the tricks

Of the trade,

Never cared how the crack came!

If you use a glass pipe,

Be sure to know how to work the flame!

Glass was the best,

Better than the rest.

White smoke, thick,

Tryna get it all,

Get it all,

My life depended on that toke.

But, damn it!

I always used too much flame!

Had to resort to the tire gauge,

Fell in love with the sound it made

When the fire hit the rock,

That snap, crackle, pop!

Rock after rock after rock,

On and on and on,

Till the crack was all gone!

Whole cigarettes burned out,

Forgot they were on.

Then comes the push,

Heat it, push it, cool it, hit it.

Repeat.

Then comes the voice

Dog, you ain't stopped yet?

Naw... not yet.

The next stage is no fun!

Down to the floor,

Looking for crumbs.

On hands and knees,

Straight trippin'!

No dope to be found,

Only paint chippins.

And when you finish,

There's a feeling of resolve,

Knowing and accepting

That the dope's all gone.

I light another cigarette,

Look out the window,

And know that this come down

Will be Hell!

I learned all of this

At the age of Twelve!

Coleridge's Middle Finger

by George Wilkerson

Sharing the name of the apartment complex around it, at perhaps a quarter mile long, Coleridge Road rammed straight through the projects. It was the crossbar between two semi-parallel streets that offered alternate routes to similar destinations, though their side roads led to completely different ends. The front one was the busy mainstream people took when speeding to Asheboro's white or blue collar districts. People motoring on it clearly had somewhere to be, somewhere to go, something to do. It was also a geographical cordon and dangerous to cross – nobody wanted to slow or stop. That intersection saw a lot of accidents. One car attempting to cross it from Coleridge got chopped in half by an SUV.

The rear street was lazier, more meandering and accommodating, but presented dangers of its own. It veined into Asheboro's darker areas where gunshots and crack pipes left blooming but distinctive scents in the air. Like many of its occupants, even the projects back there went only by a nickname, 'Low Rent', which spoke to a key feature of their character. Life itself got cheaper the deeper one went.

Like a giant middle finger flipping up from Coleridge Road into the heart of the complex, Kemp Boulevard looped about 100 yards uphill, past my apartment, where two friends and I stood sweating on a corner sidewalk. We shared a cigarette and peered downhill toward one of the other parking lots to pinpoint the tinny music that had pulled us outside to the curb – a rarely seen ice cream truck. From this distance, the kids resembled roaches as they scampered toward the sugar. Heatwaves shimmered above the asphalt, creating what appeared to be a mirage – an oasis or the birth of a metaphor for hope. Or both.

We wondered how many times it'd visit before somebody robbed it. Then we wondered whether we could trick the vendor into handing us one orange sherbet, one rainbow push-pop, and one Mickey Mouse as we pretended to dig in our pockets for money. It was 1993, hot as hell, and we were twelve and broke.

"They'd probably hand it to you... but not *us*," J, the shortest but fastest of us said, meaning – 'You're *not black*'. Puff nodded his agreement, and they both grinned. I knew the look. It teased that I looked soft, innocent – untested.

"Oh, hell, nah! I've done more stuff than both of ya'll!" I cited the fights, the stealing, the broken windows and sliced car tires. I was the most prolific.

"Well, you the one ain't been to training school," said Puff, the strongest fighter in our age bracket. He hit the dwindling cigarette.

"Only 'cause I ain't got caught like y'all." The *yet* was implicit. I felt uneasy. We all knew prison was our inevitable destination. It was a fact of life in the projects, the only life we knew how to live. Around Coleridge, people didn't dream of being doctors or lawyers or firemen... if they dreamed at all.

We all got quiet. I stubbed the cigarette butt. The ice cream truck turned onto Kemp, getting louder as it chugged up the hill and horseshoed around the bend. It became a big, boxy, yellowish riot of glittery stickers and calliopean music as it stopped in front of us. Suddenly we were jostled by a dozen excited children waving crumpled dollar bills or punching a fistful of loose change at the vendor.

My friends and I glanced at each other; they silently boosted me to attempt a free ice cream, but when I looked up, the vendor locked eyes with me and smiled. After a second he scowled and shook his head hard, as if to warn me, *'Don't you fuckin' try it kid'*. So, I didn't.

When he finally slammed and locked the serving window and pulled away from the curb, my friends and I gave chase and hopped onto the rear bumper. We clung to the panel-door seams and jumped up and down to bounce the truck, letting the driver know we were there, letting him feel our presence. Being seen and felt is its own sort of ice cream. It wasn't slowing before turning back onto Coleridge, so rather than be slung off, we hopped off and hit the ground running. We scooped up rocks and thunked them off the truck's back, laughing as it squealed its tires to gather speed toward the front street.

Though it soon disappeared, we still heard its discomfiting moon music a few moments more, until even that was gone, leaving a sticky residue in our hearts. Ice cream dreams never lasted long in Coleridge.

Coming of Age

Late adolescence is a vulnerable time,
independence is being explored, boundaries being
tested, personalities and relationships formed
while consequences are not fully comprehended.
For some, previous trauma and few protective
factors complicate an already complicated time.

A Piece Of You

by Robert Linton

Mom,

*I was in art class the first time I was suspended
from school. Another kid said, "Your momma
loves a coon," so I colored him black and blue.
Got real creative with the crayons, turned the
classroom into my playground. Yeah, it was
elementary, but that's no excuse for defending a
woman I never knew.*

*Now, here I am, severed from a lifeline that goes
back to Genesis, right before the apple fell not too
from that tree and lay there another seed. You
thought I was a blessing, so why did I grow up
thinking I was a curse?*

*House to house and far from home, too young to
understand why I was deserted – why couldn't
you give me those hugs and kisses? Teach me the
woman to love and cherish?*

*Where was my dad? Did he not think it was
important to teach a boy how to be a man? Or
did you feel this system had a better plan?*

*Let me tell you, Mom, I had to fight to be ahead of
my class, only to be graded with A-D-D and
separated from my peers. At least that is what
my therapist said right before they disguised the
drugs as Ritalin and gave me the whole
prescription, like I'm not in a school of gymnasts.
I started flipping down the wrong path. Nobody
even noticed the importance of what was missing,
until one day I showed up late for socialism,*

brought along with me the principle that there's a knowledge in wisdom for the social misfits, understandings in suspension.

I'm learning from the same corner, the one you met my father on. The only difference is that as I stand with my back to the world listening to the whispers while reading the writings on the wall, I was greeted by the hard knocks, where you're either going to stand or fall. The lesson above all, that those who choose to pave a way – rise, mastering the mind and strengthening those down on their knees, living as slaves to disease and weakness.

Mom, I'm still standing the test of time, but that's the piece of you that you passed to me. A heart that beats to its own beat. Which is why my love for blood run's soul deep, bridging the gap in my travail, building my family.

Small Wonder

by Terry Robinson

He was called Little Tee – befitting since he stood
no taller than the BMX bicycle he struggled to
mount, eager to tag along with the older kids to the
mall. His cheeks flushed, absorbing the praise,
while my friends boasted over his skill for thieving.
I knew they were manipulating him, but I didn't
speak up – being equally manipulative in my
silence. I hoped he would grow tired on our trail
and turn back, but he didn't, determination
cascading from his forehead with each trickle of

sweat. We arrived at the mall and did wheelies in
the parking lot as Little Tee vanished inside. By
the time we later headed for home, we all sported
new gold chains.

That was the first day I met Little Tee, a
burgeoning menace with an unwavering desire to
prove himself. He stole anything that wasn't
nailed down, his confidence like silk in his veins.
Thievery was only a fragment of his willingness to
fit in; one simply had to dare Little Tee. He hung
out all hours of the night, putting doubts to rest
with a fearlessness inspiring to watch.

Nights at my house were sometimes spent with
Little Tee sprawled out on the sofa or scoffing
cold-cuts and gawking at video vixens. I wondered
about his family and whether his whereabouts
were anyone's concern. He was no more than
eight or nine, and yet no one ever came looking for
him. I didn't mind that he showed up
unexpectedly and seemed to never want to leave; I
liked having him around. He had a timely sense of
humor and dreams of the future big enough to

lend me some. He gave unsparingly and never asked for anything in return. To him, charity was synonymous to wealth. Little Tee was a joy, but he *did* have a mean-streak and fought with other kids all over town like it was the latest craze. The bane of his freedom, it would earn him some stints in juvenile detention where he ultimately grew more devious.

A few years later, Little Tee transitioned from thieving to dope dealing. He hopped into cars, haggling crack rocks and turned profits with the best of 'em. He smoked cigarettes and weed, drank beers and cussed. No one seemed bothered by his youthfulness, instead they encouraged him. The more his behavior worsened, the more popular he became. By twelve years old, he had as much clientele as dealers twice his age. He was always the smallest guy on the block, but nobody had more heart.

One night Little Tee was at a local hangout when a scuffle broke out between two men with their pride at stake, one of whom had a shotgun. Scorching iron pellets ruptured Little Tee's flesh as he was inadvertently shot in the face. It would be months before he healed from his physical injuries, but his psyche hardly recovered. Suddenly, he was torn between upholding his image and breaking free from his notoriety. He had grown weary of his terrible ways, yet he couldn't break character. The truth was, the shooting ordeal changed Little Tee and heightened his conscience in a way others could never understand. He wanted so much to be done with the streets... but the streets don't always let go.

On Christmas day, December 25, 1997, I was posted up on the block when Little Tee strolled through. We greeted one another and shared some laughs before his eyes took on a piercing glare. He then let on about his dissension with rival dealers in a nearby neighborhood and asked for my help. By then, Little Tee was like a brother to me – it was all the answer he needed. Apparently, he had rented a car and parked it on Gay Street. He said he would swing by and pick

me up later. Little Tee disappeared up the street.
Some minutes later, gunshots devoured the joyous
holiday evening. Gossip raced along the streets on
the lips of hear-sayers – Little Tee was just killed
by the police!

I bolted heedlessly for Gay Street while at the same
time down a road in my head that had no end. I
kept thinking that if I got there quick enough,
maybe I could save him. I prayed the whispers
were wrong, but the look of despair on the faces of
the spectators confirmed my worst reality.
Someone was dead. "Please, God, don't let it be
Little Tee."

The shooting had taken place in the backyard
which obscured my view of the body. Rumors of
what happened ran rampant among those
gathered, igniting a bon-fire of tempers. The
ambulance arrived and carted out a body partially
covered under a blood-soaked sheet. I recognized
the sneakers and fell to the ground wailing... Little
Tee really was gone.

My Shoes

by Tevin Nero

Born and raised one of three kids by a single mom in Grand Rapids, Michigan, I struggled with who I was and tried to fit in with everybody just to feel normal, telling myself things would get better in time. Growing up, we were on welfare, struggling to live off food stamps and waiting on the third of the month to get money off our Bridge card. I had no father to turn to, or anyone to show me how to be a man. I adapted and became a part of the streets around me.

I would come home from school to no lights and no food in the house, boiling water just to take a bath. I started to stay in the streets to escape the pain of growing up in poverty and avoid watching my mother struggle. At night I would walk down the street pulling car doors to find a safe place to sleep, praying to God nobody came to the car. I would go days without meals and instead of returning home to struggle, I would go into stores and steal candy bars to survive. It eventually led to depression and wanting someone to notice me. I became a follower and before I could stop the ball from going downhill, I was in juvenile detention, praying for a blessing and direction but never really knowing if God could hear me.

I wanted more out of life and thought I had to be like everybody else to get it. I kept getting in trouble, so the state stepped in, removed me from my mother and sent me to a foster home. As soon as I got inside the home, I could tell my foster family had only taken me in for the money, and the

first chance I got, I left. A few days later I was
back in juvenile.

That was the first time I experienced depression.
Locked in my cell, I stared at the walls with
nothing but a big window and a yoga mat to sleep
on. Months later, I was released to a white foster
family. I didn't mind, but after a week I just felt
like the odd person at the table, and nobody tried
to make me feel comfortable, so I left. When I was
released, I was on lifetime probation, so when I
violated, I was sent to boot camp.

After completing the program, my life was on track
when my P.O. came and tried to send me to a
halfway house. That was the first time I noticed
the system was treating me differently than the
white kids I hung with. We were all on the same
path and case, but I would get months and they
would get days. At seventeen years, I was sent to
prison for one year and released. I was so proud of
myself for not drowning myself in weed or liquor.

And then came prison. I was walking with two
dudes, and one of them decided to take someone's
headphones. I got charged with armed robbery,
and at trial, I was found guilty of aiding and
abetting, which basically means the same charge
as the armed robbery. My case gave me fifteen to
thirty years in MDOC.

I couldn't believe I was being punished with at
least fifteen years of my life, not for being involved
in the crime, but for being around when it
happened. In 2012 I came to prison not knowing
what to expect and praying everything would be
okay. When I took my first steps on the prison
yard, I realized it was going to be a hard fifteen
years. Everybody looked at me like they were lions
and I was the prey. I ended up getting into one
fight after the other until somebody finally said to
leave me alone, and I was sent to the hole for
fighting – twenty-three-hour lockdown in a cell
with nothing but brick walls, a toilet and sink. I
was kept there for six months for defending
myself.

It was there I first wondered if anyone would miss me if I killed myself. I also decided I couldn't let this system win. I was going to do everything I could to show the world nobody's perfect, and change is possible. I started taking programs and reading business books, trying to learn something every day. It has been nine years of pain and struggle, but I like the man I've become. My goal is to now help people caught up in this system, people the world has given up on.

The Thunder of Action - A Child of Silence

by DeLaine Jones

I don't remember my mother's face. Not the
warmth of her smile or her loving embrace. In
fact, I don't have one memory of her at all. Sherly
Ann Lacey. In a drugged-out rage, my sister's
father took her life one night while she slept.
Using a shotgun, he blew her brains onto a wall.
She was due to have his second child any day.

Naturally the event devastated my, *her*, family. She was the first of my grandmother's eleven children to be lost so early in life.

Many will believe it was my mom's murder that first shaped my life, but that's not true. It was people's reaction to it that molded who I became, shaped the conclusions I would draw in life and how I'd react to pain, loss and various levels of devastation that serve as markers in every life.

Nature verses nurture? Nurture wins hands down every time. It's people who shape people. Hard scrabble environments do not create hard hearts or ill-formed souls. People do.

Louise Lacey, my grandmother, herself a quiet, *'nurtured'* woman, raised my sister and me. A beauty in her day, giving birth to eleven children by three different men, and being subject to my great-grandmother, who might well have been the basis for a character from Walter Mosely's Los Angeles, my grandmother eased into a grand-motherly figure. Love.

By the time of my mother's murder, my granny was an old hand with children. Panic after a miss-deed or the bright blood from an accident didn't send her reeling. When her brother beat his wife, she'd complain about the noise — after a while...

Hers was the knowledge of survival. Coming of age in the 40's and 50's as a black woman was as hard as it was complex. You cried when you couldn't hold it in any longer. Then you simply dusted yourself off and did the next thing needed to survive. Tough.

I'm surely being too simple, short, and impatient with the telling of her depth of spirit, her staunch faith in God and her unshakable commitment to her family. Like the moon, she's a silent force that has affected every part of me.

If my granny's footprint in life was quiet, it was only because my great grand-mother's, Josie Frederick-Hintz, was so loud. At six foot in her socks, 'Big Joe' was a demanding, sharp-tongued, physical woman. She chewed tobacco, ran a whore house and carried a .38 revolver until the day she died – not for show or as a bluff.

Born in 1911 in Louisiana, Big Joe had owned a grocery store, bowling alley, brothel, after-hours gambling den and a total of five different rental properties throughout Los Angeles. She pinned her money in a silk pouch to her bra.

Josie gave birth to two children and raised her brother's son after his murder. Systemic racism, sexism, abject poverty, rape, molestation, robbery, abuse, beatings, murder, jealous, insecure and ambitious men, their equally motivated, if shrewder, counter-parts in women – Josie not only survived it all in the big city as a veraciously stunning beauty, she was also able to, at times, win herself a few slices of pie.

But those pieces of 'white only pie' come at a cost. Josie's size in life demanded control and that others, people she loved, be smaller in life to make room for the demands of who she needed to be – the boss!

Her biological son, my great-uncle Bill, Jr., was a con who became a homosexual after being violently raped in prison. He was serving time for counterfeiting U.S. Treasury notes, five dollar bills. Her brother's son, Lemule, would become a vicious, small time pimp.

Large personalities, small egos, violent drama, they were characters you couldn't make up. My grandfather was from a cattle ranch in Texas, a pimp and hustler who discharged from the army in California.

They were all largely uneducated people save by life itself. Like the rest of us, they had flaws. The one that has been a prominent force in my life was their silence. They seemed to need to marshal their energies to hold it all in and to move forward.

Through my self-education while in prison, I've become fairly articulate, but I remember the silence of a time before I became a reader, before I saw the value of language and communication, before I learned to read, comprehend and apply ideas to further my own understanding of me, my world, my actions. Silence.

I know how the lack of the ability to express one's self in words pushes the thunder of action deep into one's ears. You're not deaf... there is no sound!

I came up in the 80's, MTV, BET, videos, PC, crack victims, empires and hip-hop culture. My family's silence was a foreign language subtitled on silent film.

Now listen! We all believe our own struggles to be the worst. It's that forest through the trees thing. But by growing up never having a single meaningful conversation with the adults in my life, I kind of raised myself. I sat waiting for something or someone to influence me, but no one ever took notice.

We are all born into motion. That's what life is — motion. A body in motion will stay in motion until it's acted upon by an equal and opposite force.

Teenagers, kids, are like vacuum chambers that suck up everything indiscriminately. Facts, emotions, ideas, words, anything floating through their lives. Sadly, sometimes, the adults who rear them contribute the most trash to the bombardment when they are the primary force policing the intake. They may sit back, looking confused and even offended as the young life bursts for lack of any meaningful release. At around thirteen to fifteen or so, they act out, rebel at the mistreatment.

Now, I grew up on violence without ever being told it was wrong to do this or that to people. Not simply the violence put forth by the men of my family and neighborhood against the women of my home and in my world, but poverty creates its own hellish acceptance of might as a viable means, be it for respect or fear.

When my father, the Baptist preacher, found out I'd been doing robberies when I'd shot and paralyzed a man – then an Assistant Attorney General to the State of Oregon – he expressed shock and hurt. "How could you do something so obviously wrong?!" I remember him blurting over the phone as I sat in a juvenile detention center.

The answer, though I didn't know how to articulate it as a seventeen-year-old, was that I really didn't know that it was all that big a deal, that people would place such a huge value on life.

That will sound twisted to some, but as a child it was *extremely* remedial to me. This may go a long way in explaining the Black Lives Matter movement to some. I'd just tried to kill *'myself'* a few months earlier. There was no panic, anger, or fear from the community. There was no rush to review the issue before various boards. As a child, I never received care or treatment for my mental health.

I'd ingested a small mountain of heart, blood pressure and pain pills. Then I got into bed. I remember passing out. Kids test the boundaries of their world. I didn't believe I wanted to deal with any more pain in my life, so as no one was ever looking, I sought to move on.

If *my* life, my *'black life'* didn't matter to the world, why would I come to the conclusion as a child that his white one did? Not that race was a factor for me or him at the time. The justice system made that point emphatically.

I was thoroughly and completely confused. As I sat in Court, it was like returning to Central Park, only to find it's been moved! You know the address, turn the corner, and it's not there! But how could you, I, be *that* wrong?

"How could I do something so obviously wrong – *'to another'*?" is the unspoken end to the question.

It's a question of value(s). Poor, uneducated black boys and girls are taught in a plethora of ways that they have little to no value. So why does it come as such a shock when their value of others falls short in word or deed?

The best lies ever told take place in the vacuum of the mind, there's no one other to refute, challenge, or evaluate them. So, speak the thought, the feeling, and force the conversation out into the 'now'. It's the thing that gives value to human beings... love spoken into a life that is loved – *valued*, even.

The Things That Remain

by Terry Robinson

Some tragedies are gradual, prolonging dismay,
others swift and unexpected, yet loss in any form
affects in us a void that can only be filled with
time. It is loss to which we are all akin, regardless
of status, color or creed, none excluded from the
woeful affliction all of humankind will suffer.
Tear-stained cheeks, fine suits and condolences
are the soothing, necessary etiquette, after which
we look to move on – but occasionally we find we
can't.

Chris was a childhood friend I grew up with on Fountain Drive, a project housing development set on the outskirts of town. There were no ills of the inner-city there, like drugs and prostitution. Sequestered by fields and lush greenery, we were burgeoning country folk. We scoured ditches for crayfish, climbed trees to pick wild berries, and explored the far reaches of the surrounding woods where we carved out a world all our own.

A favorite pastime was the community football game. Narrow eyes stared across a makeshift field as we rivaled one another. We tackled, grappled, and cussed with fervor to demonstrate our toughness, but in the end, we always left as friends, looking forward to carrying on the next day.

It was the older kids in the neighborhood that first ganged up on Chris – my brother and his closest friends. It was an assault that came without merit as Chris had committed no offense. Instead of contesting their egregious violation, Chris up and

ran away, unaware the flight-mode mentality
would begin a lifelong recurrence.

Although a rural bubble, Fountain Drive was not
the easiest place to live. No one qualified for low-
income housing more than single mothers and
senior citizens, and with many of our moms off
working to improve their conditions and the
elderly nestled up to their daytime television
shows, we ran around mostly unsupervised and
growing unrulier by the day.

We had petty differences, some escalating to fist
fights, that seldom outlasted the day. We
ransacked the neighborhood community center
and egged each other on to steal. Everything from
throwing rocks at passing cars to prank calling the
fire department, our mischief knew no bounds, yet
nothing would ignite our frenzy more than chasing
after Chris.

Chris, himself, was a passive misfit – just barely on
the right side of wrong. His misdeeds were rather
frivolous, swiping an item from a clothesline or

lifting coins for his mother's purse. He was never one to talk trash, though his size was intimidating enough. At ten, he was a head taller than most teenagers, and by thirteen, he was the same age as his shoe size. With shoulders as wide as a welcome embrace and powerful legs that were the getting-away kind, we stood almost no chance of catching him, yet we were thrilled to try.

Chris, however, was a gentle soul. He was thoughtful and forgiving, and usually, within a day or so, he was back amongst the clique. Despite his hulking size, he had a boyish quality that was much more fun to keep around, and over time, our betrayals became less frequent, until we no longer chased him away.

By fifteen, Chris' interests had matured, and he began to venture outside the neighborhood to other parts of town. It was courting girls that had procured his attention, and he thought to visit them whenever possible. However, as we had long given up chasing Chris, other kids from around town had just begun, until it seemed that bullying Chris was the most expected thing to do.

Once, I witnessed him fleeing from some guys – but did nothing in the way of help, afraid I was a word in his defense away from being bullied myself. Chris, though, had an impeccable reputation for outpacing his foes, as many of his aggressors gave chase for sport, all except one... Mikey.

A local badass who favored drinking and fighting, Mikey was the epitome of trouble. He was the guy the other bullies steered clear of. It was a brisk night outside a nightclub when Mikey set his sights on Chris – but this time, there would be no running away. Instead, Chris fought back.

As it turned out, Chris didn't run all those years because he was fearful – rather, it was a method of harm prevention. He figured as long as he didn't hurt anyone today, things would be better tomorrow. He ran away because he was being a better friend to us than we ever were to him.

Unlike Mikey, who was ruthless – not to mention a sore loser.

Some few nights later while walking home alone, Chris spotted a suspicious vehicle. He discovered that it was Mikey, along with some friends. Outnumbered, Chris had little choice but to flee, taking cover behind some houses as Mikey stepped out of the car with a gun and fired a shot in the dark. Assuming Chris was long gone, Mikey and his crew sped off, unaware the bullet had hit its mark as Chris lay dying in the night.

It wasn't until the next morning his body was discovered, entangled in the brush. Chris had been killed at just sixteen... and I never got to say, 'I'm sorry'.

Regrets, juxtapose to loss, are the things that remain, the stuff of good memories, shared experiences, and lost opportunities. After 32 years, it's regrets that have kept Chris alive in my heart, and without which, I fear I will lose one of the best people I ever knew.

A Sister's Support

by Dushaan Gillum

My sister, three years older than me, was always my best friend and biggest fan. When I was twelve she moved out of state to live with her father for two years. When she returned, she found I had transformed into someone she didn't know. I had fallen in with the bad boys and gone far astray. I was using drugs, running with a gang, and committing crimes regularly.

After my first arrest I spent several months in a juvenile detention center, thrown in an

overcrowded dormitory with kids that made me
and my buddies look like saints. It was a
concentration of the worst kids in the county,
delinquents much further along in their state of
corruption than I. It was the worst time of my life.

I left the detention center with a new attitude and
outlook on life. I decided the criminal life was not
for me. The problem was, I was stuck. I was in
debt to my gang. Not a monetary debt that could
be paid with a certain amount of cash, but a
circumstantial debt with no exact figure attached
to it. Not only had they shared their knowledge
and secrets with me, but I had accepted their
terms of life-long service upon my initiation. I was
in, and there was no easy way out.

I accepted the fact that I was stuck and sought to
simply meet the bare minimum of my obligations,
hopefully avoiding jail or death. Then our gang's
leadership decided we were to enter the illegal
drug trade. My obligations mounted along with
the list of expectations. My days became more
demanding and dangerous.

Just as I was honest with my sister about my new lifestyle, I was also honest with her about my desire to get out of the gang after my stint in detention. I once again opened up to her about our leap into narcotics sales.

My sister was seventeen and not all that experienced in the ways of the world, even less when it came to matters of the underworld. Her advice was severely limited, but she did have some interesting things to share with me about myself; a subject that she was very knowledgeable about.

I came home one night and my sister sat me down for a talk. She'd heard that some members of my gang were involved in a shooting and a rival gang was expected to retaliate. I didn't know anything about it, but I admitted it didn't matter. I didn't see any way to avoid being at risk. The only ways I knew of how to get out of the gang were to move away and never return, which was not a possibility for me, or to be kicked out for violation of a major gang rule. The latter would result in me being beaten badly and likely injured or even killed.

Tearfully, she recounted memories of me overcoming major challenges in the past. She reminded me of the trouble I had walking when I was a toddler and the braces I wore on my legs. Even at that age I was so stubborn I refused help from anyone because I wanted to master walking on my own. I used the family dog as a walker and did just that.

She reminded me of how close I came to repeating second grade because of my struggles with reading and writing. Nothing that anyone did to help worked. Eventually, I came up with my own solution, which was to divide words according to my unique way of sounding them out. I didn't repeat the second grade, and I became one of the best readers and writers in my class.

She stressed that I was a natural problem solver and assured me I would figure out a reasonable and safe way out of the gang. I wasn't so sure, but her words stuck with me.

The next day my sister gave me a bag of new clothes that she had bought with the last of her money. At that time, I wore only colors that were associated with my gang, which was not many. The clothes she bought were of an assortment of colors she purchased with faith that I would be wearing them soon. At that moment I realized what was meant by the term 'act of faith'. Her look of love and confidence was seared into my brain. Her belief ignited my creativity like nothing I'd ever imagined.

That night I awoke from my sleep with an idea, an idea that would help me be shunned by the gang without becoming their enemy. I needed to be rejected without being harmed, and the only group of people I ever saw the gang distance themselves from without any aggression were mentally impaired individuals.

The following day I instructed my sister to tell anyone who called on me that I was bedridden and in bad shape. The story was that I had smoked some marijuana that was apparently laced with something far more dangerous, and I'd seemingly lost my mind. I waited until the next day during a time when I knew most people would be out and about and emerged from the house in nothing but my underwear and stumbled in zig zags, my arms waving wildly. For days, when anyone spoke to me I drooled and simply stared off in a daze as if I didn't understand or recognize anyone. It was about two weeks into this act when my so-called friends wanted nothing to do with me.

I kept a low profile around my neighborhood and made sure to dumb myself down when any one of the gang's members were around. When summer ended and school resumed, I was living my life with no worries for my safety. I wore a wide range of colors and stayed out of trouble. Even now, when I see a rainbow or a colorful arrangement it reminds me of my sister's love and her faith in my ability.

"Boy, What's Wrong With You..."

by Louis Singleton, Jr.

"My mind was racing with thoughts I couldn't even grasp mentally. I went home and sat in the house with all the lights out, scared to move, didn't know what to do nor to say. My mom was gone to a choir convention in Mississippi during the time of the incident. While I sat in our house quietly and somberly in the front room, my mother pulled up with no clue of what just happened. When she came in the door and turned

*to lock it, I was sitting there in the dark room. I
scared her out of her wits. As a mother who knew
her child, she instantly asked me, 'Boy, what's
wrong with you sitting in here with all the lights
out?' I was so discombobulated I honestly
couldn't speak; it seemed like somebody had my
soul..."*

It's been twenty-six years for me now. I'm in
solitary confinement and have been for almost six
months. It's the first long stretch I've done in lock-
up, and I've learned if you aren't mentally strong,
it can break you. I've thought about everything
from being three years old, to that day, to this
place I am in now. I've probably aged ten years in
the last six months, but I think I've made it. My
blood pressure is crazy, but I think I've put it
under control by relaxing and focusing on better
things.

I was seventeen and still in high school when my
mom came home that night. I'd just shot at some
men. For months I'd been shot at, intimidated,
'bullied', by an adult, a man older than me. I'd sat

in a car as it was beaten with a crowbar. I'd had a gun pointed at my head. My parents knew, the school knew, the police knew. They all knew. I can never take back what happened that night.

I now understand what they mean when people talk about the school to prison pipeline. Things are a little different now in Mobile, Alabama, where I came from. I hear there are anti-bullying laws in place to protect kids like I was. There are laws to keep kids from being followed around and shot at, as well there should be. No kid should ever have to grow old in a place like this. No kid should ever be expected to know how to make people stop shooting at them.

I went from going to high school, playing football and dreaming, to living in a nightmare. No, I can't take it back. I should never have had to. It should have never gotten to that night in my living room.

Prison

The United States builds more prisons to deal with the problem of mass incarceration, facilities often plagued by staffing shortages and overcrowding, resulting in more violence and trauma for the residents, while often offering few or no treatment programs.

My First Day On Death Row

by Tony Enis

Walking into the prison felt like walking into a medieval castle at the height of the dark ages. I couldn't help but wonder if I would ever leave.

The humiliation of 'processing in' was surpassed only by my fear of the unknown. I had never been to prison, and now not only was I going to prison, but I was also going to death row, the home of men like John Wayne Gacy and the so-called 'I-57 Killer', among others.

Up until then, I had only read about such men in newspapers or saw them on television. I never, even in my worst nightmare, thought I would be counted among them, considered one of them. It was then that the reality of the situation smacked me in the face so hard I could almost feel the sting followed by the bruise. This was worse than when I came to grips with the fact that I was in a life and death situation. These men were hardened killers, and I was now among them and meant nothing to them.

At that moment, right then and there, I decided they wouldn't mean anything to me either. I was ready to do whatever I needed to do in order to survive. I hardened my heart and dismissed all thoughts of the outside world. My only reference material was movies I had seen, and in all the movies, the convict-guy acted as though the outside world didn't exist. It sounds funny now, but when you're twenty-one and have never been to prison, you cling to whatever works for you, and that worked for me.

I took a deep breath, lifted my head a little higher and walked to the cell that would be my new home. I was expecting to hear all kinds of prison noises. You know, the names and calls that always seem to happen on television when the new guy gets to prison. To my surprise (and relief), there was none of that.

I arrived at my cell, and as I was watching the key being put into the lock it all seemed to be happening in slow motion... the door sliding open... my bedroll being placed on the bunk... the door sliding shut... and the worst sound of all... the door being locked behind me.

Kenny, A Mosaic

by George Wilkerson

> *"...to remain tight*
> *in a bud*
> *was more painful*
> *than... to blossom."* – Anais Nin

To many, Kenny's a nobody – which is why he
wanted to *shine*, to prove them wrong.
Would that I could share my light with Kenny, give
him another chance
To fit in, to be normal. Since I can't, I will share

Kenny's light with you,
Break it into wafers.

Death Row, Death Throws...

We slam, we scream, we fling ourselves against
prison's cosmic ennui.
We remember life from before, our memories
another spectrum of light.
The texture of some memories never change; these
lights refuse to go
Quietly into that goodnight.
Sometimes a soul's meat-vehicle remains behind
long after the light
Has gone. Kenny remembers the moment his light
divorced his body,
Remembers when it tore itself free – remembers it
half as action sequence,
Half as background requiem for a dream. His
bodily
Memory knit together with eye-witness testimony,
here tells
You his story, sings you a history, a chorus of
blood sung

With words twinkling in air like asterisks. It was preceded
By a blinding flash of light, an insight that had sounded green,
As in the *moment is ripe*, as in... *GO*.

We all pass with varying degrees of light.

Blossom...

Perhaps the idea began as a flower — it felt like one
At the time. One of those pretty, yellow-faced ones
With white petals. Aster. Or perhaps it started as
a small star-
Like flame, a sad blue torch of forked flower in the
brain.
A risky idea one might symbolize in writing: *. An
asterisk
Indicated omission ((of common sense?)),
redaction, doubtful matters.

Portents...

−aster: a pejorative suffix denoting something
that imperfectly mimics

100

The true thing – a bootlegged or knock-off version,
for example.
–aster is also a combining form meaning 'star',
which implies
Anyone can be a star – anyone can shine like the
popular guys
Simply by stamping aster onto their chest, by
declaring, "Let me
Be light!" like in Genesis.

"dis" is a prefix meaning *asunder, part,*
away or *having a negative*
Reversing force, as in *disability*. As in *disaster*,
which is an unfavorable
Aspect of a star, emblazoned red, as in: Kenny, the
stars *do not* fucking
Align. As in: Kenny, this will rip your *asunder*,
break you apart, and
Your 'you' will go *away*... but Kenny refused to see
this light.

Men were slamming bone-yellow dominoes into
stainless steel 4-way tables,
Hollering multiples of five and clattering their

bones into position. Like built-in
Bleachers, three blocky 18-inch deep steps cut into
the rim of the day-
Room's brownish-gray concrete floor, leading
down to the lower cells.
Playing follow-the-leader exercises, acrobatic men
would balance
On the top-step's ledge, lean out with upsweeping
arms – then leap
To grab the tier's floor, to do pull-ups or show-off
by monkeying
Up, once their bodies stopped wobbling. Kenny
used to watch them,
Wishing upon those stars...

In Carnations, A Cautionary Tale...

Slow, fleshy red haloes spread
And overlap like Venn diagrams laid on cement,
Petaling around Kenny's blank comatose face
As a silken illustration of the relationship
Between grace and ground.

Soundgarden...

Light is such a fickle thing. Kenny had tried to
swing for it with a tottering
Leap.   There was a split-second grace
period. *****:
In linguistics, asterisks mark an utterance that
would be censored
By native speakers of the language. Generally a
fall
From grace is blackhole – interesting, especially
when it's a superstar.
We anticipate a comeback...   but
With us mundane asters, there is no coming back.
There
Is just a discordant **   *   ***
                    ***   **   *
        **   **   burst of asterisks that flap in the
air
Like Kenny's arms, or a flood of cusswords at
startled bus stop pigeons.
Then silence.
The very air becomes electric with prayer, or
JESUS... the name
Itself a form   of intercession. Then a meaty

thud

And a terrible revelation

Of Kenny's *horror obscurus*, his brain a pinkish-

gray

Light leaking from Kenny, after aster in brain,

after Kenny-aster

On air, after air on bone, after bone on stone.

Thunk, crack,

The genesis of a ravaged lack of all it means to be

human. A shadow

Grows from a length of gauze wrapped round and

round

A star.   That was in '97.

                              My dawg, his dog…

Every few minutes Kenny's dementia seems to

chase down his recent

History and tear chunks from its ass. I call

Kenny *my ninja*, since

I'm Asian. His cane we call *the Cadillac* to convert

limpin' to

Pimpin; his wheelchair the *Escalade* for which I

made a cardboard

Vanity plate that dangles from its back – to infuse
his disability
With style, luxury, richness. With privilege, with
ease. Nowadays
He chuckles and calls himself *stuntman
stumbles* (in his garbled drawl)
Or *Stag Lee*, a fitting confusion of Bruce Lee,
"staggering," and Stan
Lee the Marvel creator. Shit's funny, but shit
ain't *funny* funny.

                              Dark Matter...

The brain is a self-contained universe made up
mostly of star-shaped
Cells: *astrocytes*, billions and billions of them,
crackle with magic energy.
Hidden in blackness, the brain explodes with
asterisks of thought.
It is the seat of language, music, motion...
personality. A lump
Of grace that will shine until we die, but...
sometimes
Stars flicker and wink out, entire galaxies have

power outages,

And the wrinkled surface of the deep becomes

void: dementia

Steals the self. It would be simpler if one just

vanished

The sun – not this gradual decay into the sightless

realm where darkness is

      awake upon the dark.

Six Cubic Feet

by George Wilkerson

As a Boy Scout grasping the basics of wilderness survival and hiking through buzzing, mosquito-infested forests while life as I knew it faded behind, I first had to grapple with transience and the pain and fear interwoven with impermanence. Everything I carried served a practical function, and after being rolled up, tucked, folded, stacked and packed, it altogether occupied six cubic feet, or so my canvas rucksack advertised.

An object's value was the sum of its utility minus its volume and mass, measured in cubic inches and ounces. The less I had, the freer I felt. My sense of liberty kindled when I was limited to basic necessities, my creativity sparked to life by the demands of simple survival. One of my handiest items was twine, a fat spool of the sturdy kind for starting fires, building snares, catching fish, dangling food from a tree branch, wrapping tourniquets, and generally for binding. Many things find a higher purpose when bound.

Now I camp in a cell with the square footage of a tent. According to prison policy, I should be able to fold tuck, roll, stack and pack all my belongings into three boxy, flimsy, white plastic shopping bags about the size of brown paper grocery bags, all amounting to a total of six cubic feet.

Books qualify as personal property, no more than ten. It takes ten books to adequately study my faith, but it also takes ten law books to adequately work on my legal appeals and get my body off death row. That's 2.5 cubic feet of mental and spiritual acuity for me.

I own one cubic foot of hygiene items, luxuries to prevent odors, rashes and to preserve dignity, to soothe my itchy need to feel neat and clean. Two more cubic feet are crammed with my creativity – paper, pens, poetry, essays, drawings, notebooks full of ideas.

That leaves half a cubic foot for commissary food and sentimentality. I own a large brown envelope packed with tattered pages scrawled on by my dad before he died and crappy-but-cute kindergarten drawings by my nieces who swear I'm the world's best uncle even though I was already here when they were born. I also have a two-inch stack of photos of my brothers and me when we were little boys, of our parents prior to their divorce, of people I've never met and places I've never been but that are important to my friends or family and therefore important to me.

That's how I fill and maintain my six feet of cubic space, carved from a hard place. Technically, then, my commissary food is actually considered contraband and could be confiscated. To keep anything new is to discard something old.

I keep my life packed up in bags that tear easily, which is fine by me. In the end my real treasures – my faith, my memory, my love and my creativity – they all inhabit the infinite space inside my soul, incorruptible, ethereal, eternal... and free to bloom.

Arriving On Death Row

by Charles Mamou, Jr.

My thought – *'My life is over'*. No more clothes, parties, women, vacations. No more freedom and all that joyously came with it. As we drove, I noticed beer trucks zoom past. Commuters drove by without a care as to why the ornery white van was even on the same highway as their colorful vehicle.

As I began to reflect, the silence became revealing. I noticed things I would've missed under other circumstances. My senses adapted with a sense of urgency. I knew the van's muffler had to be busted because it made a hissing and popping noise every 45 seconds or whenever we slowed down and sped up again. I noticed when the driver loudly belched twice and gave a hearty laugh. The van's radio was tuned to a country station, playing songs like Smoke Rings In The Dark and You Don't Impress Me Much. The singer had a hook that stuck in my mind – 'Who do you think you are? Brad Pitt?' It was a braggadocious melody that I actually liked, even though I didn't have a clue who Brad Pitt was.

At our first stop I was handed over to TDCJ prison officials. One of the officers looked like Boss Hog from the Dukes of Hazard, just taller. He gave the deputies a solid handshake before exchanging a few words and gestures in a code that only they could understand. "Na, look here. Can you read, boy?" the prison guard asked me in a gauche southern plantation owner's drawl that made me sick in the ears. At this point I was so emotionally drained that I felt faint. I was broken, and I didn't even realize it. I answered him by nodding my head 'yes'.

"A'ight. Na, we'se gonna take you inside and get you processed in our system. It's only gonna be two ways it'll happen. One. You act like a man, and we treat you like one. Or, two. Act like a ass, and we'll f!@# you like one. Is we clear?"

Again, I nodded my head 'yes'.

They took my chains and handcuffs off without a care of me attacking them. The guards seemed comfortable around the convicted, as if they'd accepted the idea that they were simply 'inmates' too, except they were getting paid to be there. Or their ease could've been due to the guard towers that held gunmen inside with their rifles aimed at me, ready to shoot with any sign of a snafu that I might cause.

I followed behind them, and when we entered the huge crimson brick building one of the guards yelled an introduction that was louder than a

bullhorn, getting the attention of the other sixty or
so inmates and officers. "Dead man walking! Get
y'all faces against the wall!"

Prison policy demands that all non-death row
inmates are supposed to face the wall in a frisk
position, not looking at any death row inmate as
one passes by. Why? I have no clue – makes no
sense to me. As I passed by, some inmates stole
glances at me. Some had sympathetic eyes.
Others were only frustrated that my arrival had
delayed them momentarily from getting to where
they wanted to be.

I was placed in a bullpen that smelled of bleach.
The floor shined from being freshly buffed. Again,
I was ordered to strip nude, hand over the county's
orange uniform that I had worn, and given an off-
white jumpsuit with 'DR' painted on it. Then I was
quickly ushered to an awaiting barber's chair
where the baby afro I was beginning to admire was
cut into an uneven buzz cut. "Standard prison
haircut. Sorry," the inmate barber explained.

Once that was over I was brought before the classification officer. He looked like a thin, 60-year-old liberal and impressed me as educated and reasonable. He smiled at me, which was a welcome sight, and directed me to sit down. After taking a seat I learned that looks are quite deceiving. As it turned out, the man was the most disrespectful officer I met that day.

"You know, in my day *your kind* would've never gotten so much generous attention. We simply would've brought you out yonder, found a good ole tree to hang ya from. Just one less..." he was saying just before he cut himself off, not finishing his racist insult. He was about to say the almighty peccant N-word that has divided whites and blacks from the moment it was conceived for the sole purpose of pejorative dehumanization – but he didn't. He didn't have to. It was already understood who and what he was.

He would go on to ask me a bunch of questions that he fed into his computer. Questions like, "With a name like Mamou, what, you Muslim?"

pronouncing the 's' like a swarm of 'z's, in an effort
to insult the religion.

"No. I'm from Louisiana." And even though I had
no previous religion, I told him I was a Christian –
because that's what my mom said would set me
free. I would later find out that in 1999, Texas sent
48 men and women to death row. That was the
most ever sentenced in a single year, which many
defense lawyers would say indicates DA's abused
their power and overcharged the poor and
minorities just to stay true to their tough on crime
stance.

As soon as the interrogation was over, I was loaded
into another van. This one had no window, and
the guards were two redneck hillbillies that drove
like NASCAR drivers down the non-scenic back
roads with their music blasting to an R&B/Rap
station. I just knew we were destined to get into a
wreck. We sped over humps and nearly ran over a
three-legged dog as we made our way around
sharp curves, knocking me to the floor several
times. It took about an hour before we pulled up

to the back entrance of the Ellis One prison. Like so many before me, I knew nothing of the process or what to expect once I exited the van. I didn't know anything about appeals. All I thought about at that moment was that I was about to face the executioner.

I was quickly escorted through the general population showering area, where a hundred obsequious nude inmates stood in line to take a quick shower. I recall thinking that the margin of error of one inmate rubbing up against the backside of another was extremely tight. I told myself, *'If this is how death row inmates shower, I'll be one smelly dude.'*

I kept my face straight ahead, not allowing my curiosity to invade their privacy. The walk was quick and then that damn announcement rang out again as we entered the main hallway, "Dead man walking! Hit the wall, you maggots!" The officer barking the order tightly gripped his steel club stick, eager to beat back any inmate that wasn't in compliance. Again, the inmates faced the wall, noses touching brick, hands and legs spread. I felt bad that so much attention was being placed on me, causing these incarcerated men more humiliation. As soon as we passed, they continued doing what they were doing as if I'd never walked by.

We reached the housing area where death row inmates were held, and my body alerted me that it had been an entire day and a half since I'd eaten anything. I was famished. I was brought to J-21's wing and there on the floor by the entrance was a blue food tray with what appeared to be a perfectly uneaten piece of baked chicken. My mouth began to salivate in ways that were unnatural to me because I'd never experienced that kind of hunger before. I wanted that chicken so badly I didn't care about the self-imposed dignity I'd conjured up about being a Mamou. Mamous don't cry, we don't beg, we don't embarrass ourselves in public, we are to act regal even if we aren't. Well, hunger pains are a callous dictator too, and I would have dropped to my knees and lapped that meat up with my mouth like a dog had they told me I could. I informed the guards I was extremely hungry. They smiled, checked the time on their watches and told me that chow would be served shortly.

It would be two hours before 'chow time' came. In the meantime I was brought to a cell that reminded me of an ecosystem of grime, filth, germs, critters, graffiti and loneliness. There was a banal smell that hung in the air.

At around 4:30 they brought us 'chow', which consisted of what they called tuna-pea-casserole. I'd never heard of anything like it. I tasted it, taking in a huge chunk, gagged and immediately threw up. Prison food smells and tastes different in a way that alarms your body as it enters. Natural defenses go up and try to eject the invasion. It takes months to get acclimated to the taste of half cooked foods, that are at times spoiled or not food at all.

All the TVs were on, and the rest of the guys were glued to the cartoon show on Fox called Beast

Wars. I thought that was too immature for me, so I sat on my bunk. I was hungry, frustrated and angry. I threw my crying face into my hands with my mouth trembling, silently whispering a prayer to this God my mother prayed to, languidly mouthing, "I can't do this sh**!"

The Hole

by Chiron Francis

Day One (Down I Go)

I wake to something crawling on my face, instinctively removing what feels like a very large cockroach as pain jolts through my shoulder and the part of my face I just touched. One of my nostrils is clogged up making it hard to breathe. As I exhale through my mouth, I feel the numbness of my lip. Dried blood has partially sealed my mouth and nose shut. My top lip is twice as large as normal. I ignore the pain in my shoulder, which has now turned into a throbbing headache. I place my hand on the part of my head that hurts the most. My head also seems to have grown twice as large since I last touched it. *Now, I remember.* All that guard had to do was *ask* me to leave the chow hall, he didn't have to put his hands on me. In that moment when I pushed him away, I forgot the first prison rule I learned when I got here – *never* touch the correction officer.

Day Three

'Does the light above my head ever go off?' Over time, I learn it doesn't, serving to assist the guards who pass my cell see inside. They are able to view me through a small square window located on the only door to this hole.

I hear familiar keys jangle and know a guard is in the hall making rounds. Before I can debate with myself what kind of round it is, I hear a man announce, "Chow time!" Shortly after that I hear the bean slot drop open. The slot is located a few feet below the rectangular window and is where everything from food to mail is passed to a person in solitary confinement. These items also come as a privilege. Because I assaulted an officer, my mail is withheld, probably destroyed. My food is also special. I'm given 'food loaf', an all-in-one baked bundle of whatever is being served that day.

As I listen to the bean slots open down the hall, I know they are near. I wait in eager anticipation. I'm hungry and food loaf is better than no loaf. Like magic, my slot is opened and presto, food loaf and a paper plate with a plastic spork appear. I quickly grab it and wait for the liquid beverage that will accompany my meal. It too will be savored. Just then, the guy in the next cell decides to 'jack the slot', which is sticking a body part out of the slot and refusing to remove it. The guard delivering the food immediately asks the offender to remove his arm from the slot. The offender responds with obscenities and an audible spit. The officer radios for backup, who quickly arrive in a musical symphony of key jangles. Commands are shouted to the offender, "Offender, remove your arm from the slot!" I try to see through the square window what's going on, but my efforts are vanquished by an officer who sees my face and abruptly closes the small square door mounted over the window. Then I hear an audible 'whap', a scream from the offender, something about 'you broke my arm', followed by more obscenities. And just as quickly as it all started, it was over. Later that night, I hear the offender next to me whimpering about how the guard broke his arm, and how he's going to sue them and their mothers.

'Good luck with that, pal. This is Texas.'

Day Seven

I try talking to the guy next door through the wall and quickly determine he is mentally unstable. He talks to himself or some imaginary being in his cell and makes strange noises with an unknown body part. He laughs uncontrollably a lot.

I, in my boredom, have managed to count all the cracks in the wall and floor of my cell. I've even managed to make out imaginary images such as demons, women and what can only be described as mythical creatures, all derived from splotches on the wall. I've asked for a book, but as of today – nothing.

Day Fourteen (Sanity Slip)

I'm given a book. It is delivered by a very attractive female guard. Her perfume reminds me of the companionship of a woman. I speak to her, and she seems to still have some compassion left in her. I won't see her again.

The book is 647 pages of kickass action. The author is some guy named Greg Hurwitz who has written several books about some badass orphan. I've never read a book as fast. I consider reading it again, but what's the point? I already know the ending. Still no word on when I'll be getting out of here. I workout and pray daily. I also reflect on my actions and how I got stuck in this hole. Simple things that so many take for granted are essential to maintain my sanity. I crave a look at the night sky and glimpse of the moon and stars. A breath of fresh air, even exhaust fumes, would be welcome in this new world.

I wonder how my mother is doing. I know she must be worried sick about me, especially since I have not been able to call or write. Maybe she will call the prison and inquire about my well-being.

The laughter next door becomes contagious. It's not laughter of joy.

Day Twenty-One

I've been given a blanket to cover up with, which does nothing to combat the cold temperatures. The blanket is made of the exact same fabric used to cover speaker boxes or upholster the trunk of a car. It's getting rough in here. I remember when I was a child and how I used a blanket as protection. Protection from the boogyman. Who was this boogyman, that mysterious monster-man who hid under children's beds, in closets and in the dark shadowy corners of bedrooms? Where

did he go in the day? Was it a place like this? Was
the man next door him, the one who rocks me to
sleep with his screams and laughter? Am I the
boogyman?

Day Forty-Two (Suicidally Seduced)

I've started talking aloud to myself. I remember
what my mother used to say about talking to
yourself. *"You're not crazy if you talk to yourself,
unless you start answering yourself. I can't
remember if I've ever done that, have I? No, I
haven't."*

Thoughts of my wife and son out there in that
cruel world eat at my heart. I grasp at my chest to
quench the pounding crunch of my need to know
they're okay. All I can do is believe they are. Then
a thought from out of nowhere comes into my
mind. What if I end my life? For sure all my
troubles will be over...

I start to devise a plan on how I can do it. I can
easily tie the blanket around my neck, tight

enough to cut off my oxygen. I attempt this by straightening the blanket out and twisting it into a rope. I then wrap that around my neck and tie a knot. When I'm done, I realize I've wrapped my nose and mouth in my attempt. Death by suffocation, not strangulation. Halfway through my desperate act, something inside my head tells me, *'This is not the way.'* If I kill myself, what will they tell my son? If I kill myself, the Texas Judicial System has won the game.

The blanket soon starts to itch my face. Torturing myself before I die is definitely not the way to go. I unravel the blanket from around my head, ball it up and toss it in the corner. Later on in the night, I retrieve the blanket from the corner and fold it into a makeshift pillow. Despite the freezing temperature, I sleep and dream myself out of the hole.

Day Forty-Three (Small Glimpse of Hope)

I awake discombobulated. It takes me some time to realize my breakfast is sitting on the floor of my cell. Someone has opened my cell door, and I was totally unaware. I pick it up and place it on the sink, which also serves as a table. I try to go back to sleep but it is impossible. I get up and perform my daily routine of washing up and exercise. After two hours of strenuous calisthenics, I sit on the floor and meditate, thinking about my time in the hole and all I've been going through, mentally and spiritually. As I reflect on those things, I feel something crawl across my leg. I then realize I am sitting in a line of marching ants. *'How did they get in here?'*

I follow their path to a small hole where the floor meets the wall. It dawns on me. This place that was designed to restrain and isolate me, could also be my way out in the form of convincing myself that if I can survive *this* environment, I can survive anything this prison throws at me...

Small World

by Terry Robinson

A boundless void, daunting and ever present, a
place where even the pleasure of a night's dream is
wrecked by the reality of the waking day – that's
where I live. It's a domain that spans a mere 6×10
feet, made of menacing concrete and steel, and
offers the barest resources within an atmosphere
that effects only sorrow. That's life on Death Row,
rankled daily by restrictions... told what to do, how
to dress and when and where to go with little
choice but to comply, dutifully denied the simplest

liberties many folks take for granted and yet the real punishment seldom comes by day, rearing its head most often at night.

IU240 are the numbers of my prison cell, a crypt of sorts, where memories are elicited and misery reserved. With twenty years of digital sequences like IU240 to mark my identity, I am a nameless statistic with nothing left in the world to call my own. The days here are but a tireless effort to distract from Death Row – tabletops, TV, books and gossip, anything to cope with the pain. Yet 'Lock Down' call begins an agony anew, one from which there are no delusions or escape.

IU240, a paltry wasteland of fussy dust mites that gather in hard-to-reach places. Lonely, except for the crowd of tender thoughts that threaten to devour my complacency. "Stand clear!" the warning blares as the mechanical gears churn and the vaulted door slams shut while I struggle to regard IU240 as a sanctuary rather than something worse than death.

The nights number 7300 that I've spent in isolation. My voice yearns for companionship, but the solitude is stifling, the air bland and smells nothing of freedom, more of apathy. As the brightness in the room plummets, I cling to a reason to steady the light within. I am afraid in the dark I may lose my way. Trivial items that lie dormant by day are now crawling reminders of the oppression, making rest and peace of mind laborious and evasive.

There is a column of tissue rolls stacked in the corner that serves as a coffee table and a desk constructed from Maruchan soup boxes and shoddy adhesive. Bed sheets suspended from paper clips along the walls are all there is for privacy, yet in a world of trash where there is hardly treasure, one must improvise. There's a stainless-steel mirror that erredly reflects the stains of my past transgressions, a toilet that ticks tauntingly and faucet water that tastes like lead. The concrete and steel with an eerie affinity to that of the blood and spirit of the many who have perished already and those who await their fate.

It is likely I will die in prison, a truth that is written on the age lines of my face. Already twenty years of my life's essence etched into the fabric of these walls, and yet, IU240 isn't some infamous badland where hope doesn't exist. It doesn't stand in the way of accepting responsibility and the effort to amend wrongs.

On the contrary, it's a place where accountability offers temperance and renewal... a place where I have emerged from chaos a better person than when I arrived.

What Am I Doing In Here?

by DeLaine Jones

It's the look in his eyes as he spits some slick disrespect in my face, not bothering to stop at my cell, casually flaunting his freedom. It shouldn't come as a surprise to me. It was such seemingly casual violence on my part that saw me into a cage after all.

But the sting of helplessness, of a raw, exposed nerve, the vulnerability, leaves a metallic, blood-like taste in my mouth, slashes at my soul... It's a feeling I quickly cover with splashes of rage, the most potent form of emotion I can find. Funny that it lives next door to passion and across from love in me.

It's a child's reaction to the inability to deal with a moral responsibility seeking to overwhelm me, to rise in me until it covers my nose and I can't breath for the insanity in my mind... a refuge denied to a man with a gun in his face.

The greater the fear, the thicker the lid of the angry outburst needs to be to hold it down, the fear of being at another's mercy, subject to their whims, their madness.

This is what people felt when a kid stuck a gun in their faces and took their money, their freedom, boldly stomping through their lives as if they didn't matter. Was my stride the same as George Zimmerman's, the officers', the guards'? Did I have the same 'fuck you' strut and that same look in my eyes?

"It ain't no fun when the rabbit's got the gun."

I fall back on my bunk, into the prison of my life, swallowing the taste in my mouth. Life is about the connections you make, if and when you are able to put the pieces together. An I.Q. test measures how quickly a person can pick up a concept, make a connection, spot a pattern. Is there a test to show whether someone cares enough to make the attempt? That info seems more valuable to me somehow.

This isn't who or where I wanted to be, living within circles within circles of violence, violence with no goal of shaping me into the dreams of my grandmother, my father.

Change. That's what's left after trans-for-mation. No matter what I change, or who or what I forge myself into, the things that truly confine my life will not budge. They're built to outlast me. Despair? No, reality.

Hear me. Most people live in a world of 'potential'. Some one(s) planned on me being in this cage more than eighty years before I was born. How do I change that? How did they know that I would shoot that white man? That my seventeen-year-old black face wouldn't be remembered by him in either rage or fear?

In the face of such forgiveness, how could I fail to forgive the guard? His ignorance hadn't left me with a bullet in my spine, unable to walk or live without pain. I couldn't say the same for my own.

Moral culpability is the substance that adulthood is made of, the mortar that binds the actions of our lives together like so many river stones. But the energy of such a powerful emotion – rage – doesn't simply evaporate under the heat of responsibility. It was only then, after I pulled that trigger, that I recognized the extreme danger – Quicksand!

This is where brown boys who are guilty get reduced to numbers in boxes, like lotto balls, to

consume what is left of themselves. It happens in
secret – a private meal washed down with a
grandmother's tears, as the child she loves
crumbles under the weight of a basketball score in
years.

That's all that was left after I sacrificed my
childhood's hopes with the blast that shattered
multiple lives, only to rise like smoke on the winds
of reason. I couldn't to this day tell you why I
pulled the trigger. Reason will ever be the enemy
of children.

It's what was left after the white D.A. and my white
attorney saw a seventeen-year-old brown boy
agree to plead guilty and to ninety years in prison.

It's what was left after the white judge refused to
find anything redeemable in my childish eyes. I
was guilty, nothing more.

What is left is twisted into this callous on my soul.
Armor. A thickening of the skin, instinctively
grown to protect the child in me from what I'd

done – what was being done to me. An act that none of the only white faces, save my three people, in the courtroom seemed to look interested in, watching the judge hand down a ninety-year sentence for a non-homicide offense to the brown kid that I was.

Should race have excused or defended me? *Never.* But when the lines of brown boys waiting to be sent to prison by predominantly angry white judges stretches into the horizon... and has done for decades...

If you are looking for the stereotypical black rage found in the ink of most prison pens that allows one to dismiss the words as broken, to look away from the destruction by fire of brown skinned boys measured not by the love and mercy due a child at their worst but in metric tons – this is not that.

To not look away is to *see*, to see is to *know*, and to know as an adult makes us morally culpable to act. Adults should expect the morals of their justice system to reflect their own values. It's the only way the American system works.

There are white people standing with the black lives movement, armed with their own rage at what they have seen and know to be deadly and murderously wrong with what is being reflected back from our justice system. "What are they doing out there?" is what some ask. What should be asked now that they've seen and know is, *"What am I doing in here?"*

It's what I ask myself every day.

The Kiss I'll Never Forget

by Charles Mamou, Jr.

I will never forget August 30, 2006. I was on A-pod, occupying B-dayroom's recreational section, nexus to Death Watch on Texas Death Row. It was after 5:30 p.m. and visitation was over, so I headed toward the front of the dayroom, hoping to catch a guy I affectionately called Road Dawg. His real name was Derrick Frazier, but many knew him as Hasan. Before that, he was Castro – like Fidel, Cuba's former dictator.

Hasan never knew his father. His mother left when he was fifteen, weeks later to be found dead of a drug overdose. He had an abusive stepfather. Eventually, Hasan grew tired of the abuse and ran away. He began living in the streets and soon after was adopted by Crip gang members. Becoming a new member meant he had to get a new name, and that's how Castro was born.

I didn't meet Castro until after he arrived on Texas Death Row. It was then that he denounced his gang, took up religion and became a Muslim. He studied the religion relentlessly, renaming himself Hasan and following the ways of Islam. He founded two newsletters – Operation L.I.F.E. and the Texas Chapter of the Human Rights Coalition, and that is how I came to know him. Hasan took his money from that and practiced 'zakat' towards his fellow death row inmates, no matter what race or religion. If you didn't have, he gave clandestinely.

When he told me he had received an execution date, he said it as if he was telling me the score to a football game that I had missed, there was no emotion – at least, none on the outside. He told me he was going to unroll his mat and pray... and he did.

Hasan had a friend from Canada that was seeing him through visits. He even had her visit me. He was visiting with her on August 30, 2006, as I stood in the dayroom waiting to get a glimpse of him, to somehow communicate my solidarity through a look I planned on giving him. Shortly after 5:30 that evening he came walking through the door, looking like a king who stared down adversaries without an ounce of fear. He hadn't noticed me, so I called out to him. Robotically, he turned my way, and seeing me, broke free from the escorting officers' grips and started my way. He was handcuffed, and the guards didn't stop him. I had no idea what I was going to do, but I stuck my hands out of the bars and gave him a hug. He began to cry, tears that fell rapidly, knowing time was running out.

Then he kissed my left cheek, whispering into my ear, "Road Dawg, do me a favor. You have the best chance of any of us here. Get free. Go home. Don't let these folks win. Promise me!"

I told him nothing. Not that I didn't want to. I was still shocked he kissed me, and at the same time the guards started calling his name and came to retrieve him to bring him into the 'death watch' cell. It all happened so fast, words eluded me, and I watched my friend walk off.

That night I was standing in the door of my cell, all the lights off on the pod, when I became aware of something I was seeing. If I looked at the pod's control picket that is made of glass, I could see the reflection of all the cells on death watch, and I turned my attention to #8 cell, which held Hasan. There he was, standing in the door with his light on. His light was on. Mine was off. I watched him for a few hours. He didn't move once. Through the years I wondered what he was looking at. Was he soaking in his last hours of life as he looked out in the dark jungle of iron bars and steel gates?

Trying to understand how he came to his final moments? Was he waiting and hoping for a miracle? Or was he wondering what was I doing standing in my cell's door in the dark? Did he see me? Eventually, I went to lay down. I said a prayer for my friend and would get up to come to the door every so often only to see him still standing there.

Hasan left at 7:40 a.m. for his last few hours of visitation with his friend from Canada. I also was told that an aunt came to see him. He never came back.

When they pronounced him dead a little after 6:30 that evening, I cried, unconsciously holding the cheek he'd kissed. My friend was the epitome of change, strength, and courage. I will never forget that about him.

Transience

by George Wilkerson

A few years ago, here on Death Row, a handful of men were summoned to our unit manager's office. They didn't return for weeks. Prison administrators accused the men of plotting... something that was never explained. All we knew was that the guys, our friends, were put in segregation while being 'investigated'. They returned a couple weeks later after nothing turned up, a few pounds lighter physically and also in terms of their property.

Putting a prisoner 'under investigation' is the prison's way of segregating him without charging him, without writing him up for an infraction, without due process. It's a way to punish in advance while searching for a legitimate reason to justify a formal write-up. It's a discretionary tool administered in response to rumors or suspicion of a rule violation, vengeance, say, for pissing off a duty lieutenant.

Prisons are highly structured, highly controlled environments, governed by routine, every day much the same as the food – bland, monotonous, repetitive. You'd think being permanently imprisoned would mean where a person lays their head would be set in stone, right? Despite control mechanisms shaping nearly every facet of daily life, being incarcerated means shit can happen at any second. No one can be sure where they will sleep at night – their current cell, bandaged on a hospital bed, shivering in a psyche ward, handcuffed in a holding tank, waiting for a cell assignment in solitary. And anytime someone is forced to move off the unit, their personal property is searched and held to the strictest standard. Extra anything equals contraband.

Every time we get sent to the hole, we lose our personal property. Our jailers, tasked with packing our belongings for these moves, say much of our property is 'contraband' because it 'exceeds space limitations'.

Right before I came here in '06, someone wrote an anonymous note on one of the guys already here. The staff despised him, and he was accused of bullying the men on his pod. Though no one ever came forward with evidence or testimony to substantiate this claim, he was placed 'under investigation' and didn't return for years.

Once you are in solitary confinement, if you violate even the most trivial policy – having an extra pair of socks, things that typically go ignored or at worst elicit a verbal warning – you earn additional write-ups. Fifteen days. Thirty days. Forty-five days. Days pile onto your stay. Receiving a series of write-ups in quick succession can get you recommended for long-term isolation, a minimum of six months but usually at least a year.

Another time, while awaiting my trial, officers raided the cell next to mine. Through an interconnected air vent, I heard the officers informing the irate and disbelieving occupant that they had to take all of his property, including the clothes he had on, because he was being put on suicide watch. I never found out whom he'd offended, but somebody – a prisoner or staff member – had filled out a sick-call in his name, posing as him and threatening to kill himself. He was forcefully stripped naked and dragged to an observation cell on the psych ward, where he spent the next two weeks.

Incarcerated people accumulate a ton of attachments, possessions, sentiments, activities, etc. We latch onto them, make them a part of us, become dependent on them. They make us heavy. For that reason, many guys in here walk around high-strung and hyper vigilant about their interaction with staff, "Man, I won't even speak to that officer. He's too spiteful. I don't want him searching my cell – I've got too many books." Or photos. Or art supplies. Or food. Any time I'm called to the office for an appointment or to pick up legal mail, my heart races. I question whether I've pissed off anyone, I wonder if I'll return.

Before officers enter our area to search cells or arrest someone, they stop in the hall at the guard booth and start putting on blue latex gloves like nurses wear. We watch through the Plexiglas wall. Someone will holler, "MAN DOWN!" and during the fifteen seconds prior to the guards' entrance, we ask ourselves, "Who are they coming to get? Did they glance up at my cell?"

Several toilets will flush, swallowing… whatever. Most of us prop ourselves in doorways, or continue what we were doing in the dayroom, watching but not watching TV, playing but not playing chess, stiff but nonchalant, not wanting to draw attention to ourselves in case the guards are undecided about who they are coming for.

Some guys are sentimental hoarders, their cells
thick with excesses of everything. Others keep
nothing. Other than a cup, toothbrush,
toothpaste, bar of soap, and neatly made bunk,
their cells hardly look occupied. They give the
guards nothing to hurt them with, no leverage.
They're nearly invisible and are impervious to
prison life.

Incarceration has a transient quality, akin to
homelessness, forcing us to continually determine
which of our possessions are extra baggage. And,
how do I avoid the unavoidable and
unpredictable? I don't. I simply prepare for it.

Class of 99: Day 3...

by Charles Mamou, Jr.

It's all a dream. Or is it?

Something was off, I could sense it. It looked like Madear's home, it just didn't *feel* like her home. I could hear a familiar hymn being sung sotto voce towards the side of her home where her adjacent storage building was. She kept her washer and dryer there. She also had two extra freezers in there holding tons of assorted meats. Sodas were stacked to one side of the wall as high as five-feet, and gallons of assorted juices lined the floor.

Madear loved buying in bulk because she loved to cook and feed others. There was an area opposite the beverages where all her holiday decorations were kept – including a unique white crystal four-foot holiday colored Christmas tree she proudly displayed in her window every year. To this day I've never seen anything like it. It was also the place I first kissed a girl, Carla Landry, and I liked it!

This area was not huge by any standard, but my little brother and some of my friends often used the washhouse, as we called it, as a club house. Madear would be there daily, putting loads of clothes in to wash, and once dried, she would fold and inspect to see if the whites were white enough or if the colored clothes were bright enough. She had no problem rewashing the clothes until they met her satisfaction.

So, it wasn't odd to find her inside. I rushed through the door and saw her rocking away in her hand-crafted wooden rocking chair that she used to find her Zen-moments in, relaxing or simply contemplating what she would do next. Madear didn't speak much. I never heard her raise her voice, but she always evaluated any situation before acting, and when she did speak, her observations or opinions were always thought-out.

I could not see the features of her face, no eyes, mouth or lips – nothing. There was nothing but warm, blinding light. The rest of her body, from the neck down, was there. Even her favorite sundress graced the length of her body. She rocked away, faster than I recalled her doing. I tried to advance closer, but I could not move. It was as if I was stuck in cement that had long since dried, my feet buried.

"Don't worry, Baby. Everything will be fine. You'll see. You'll be fine," she repeated. Her voice sounded as if she was speaking to me from behind a waterfall... though soothing and comforting. I wanted to lay my head on her lap, allowing her to pat and massage me the way one would do a cat. Her voice brought about a sense of conviction to my soul. I could feel tears, hot tears, running down my cheeks. My heart started to beat more urgently. I blinked for a second and Madear and her rocking chair started fading away in the pasture behind her home. She faded the way a home run baseball floats away... and is gone.

"Chow time, maggots! Get your asses up if ya'll wanta eats!" barked a guard.

'Fuck!' Steel gates crashed into more steel. *'It was all a dream? A stupid, fucking dream!?!'* The mist of tears I had shed were still damp on my cheeks. My heart was still thumping. I turned over to see what time it was, fifteen minutes after three in the morning. I'm not a morning person and my weakness was affirmation of that as I turned on the cell's light. I'm not a breakfast eater either, and I was going to refuse because it was too early to be eating, but the growling sounds coming from my empty stomach were the motivation I needed to eat something. I was hungry. No, I was starving, having eaten little to nothing my first few days on the famous Texas Death Row. Pancakes were served. They were not IHOP worthy, but I

wasn't going to be picky. I was also given an 8-ounce carton of milk, a 4-ounce carton of orange juice and four spoons of fruit cocktail. I ate everything before going back to sleep, hoping I wouldn't dream again.

Around ten o-clock in the morning an officer opened the bean slot to the cell and threw a big commissary bag in, "Some of your fellow-condemned brothers put some things together for ya."

I stared, my eyes fixed on him, wondering if he was joking. I don't know if I expected a snake to crawl from the bag or a bomb to go off at any moment. Sure, I was paranoid. This wasn't Kansas anymore. I didn't know what 'this' was.

After some time, I got up, kicked the bag a little, and waited for a reaction. Nothing. I gently opened the bag to find a bunch of snacks, four writing tablets, envelopes, and over fifty bucks in stamps which, due to my naiveté, I used to tape photos of my children to the walls. I had no idea I was supposed to use stamps to write. No shit. I hadn't written a letter to anyone at that point. I communicated through daily phone calls or visits. There were socks, a thermal top, and some much needed hygiene products, all of which I greatly appreciated. No note was given. No one shouted to get my attention. Nothing. The act of charity was empathetically done. Guys knew I was going through some things because they went through the same 'new beginning'. It was an act of kindness I greatly appreciated even though I had no one to thank.

I walked to the front of the cell to look out. The place was teeming with sounds of existence, a farrago of inmate laughter, crashing steel, buzzing light fixtures that looked like something you'd expect to see in the beginning of the 20th century, as well as radios and multiple televisions that blared recklessly. This 'new world', was too much for me to embrace, so I returned and sat on my bunk. I grabbed photos of my children and their mothers, my mother and siblings, and I thought

about what they were going through. I loved them
all dearly, and the more I thought about them, the
more I cried. I saw an unopened letter I had
received the night before. It was from one of my
children's mothers. It started off like a Dear John
letter. She was telling me she was getting married
to a truck driver. A year earlier I shared a bed with
her. I immediately thought, *'Where the fuck did he
come from?'* At that moment, I was certain. I was
no longer dreaming.

"In The Interest of Justice"

Mandatory minimums and overly harsh sentencing often leave many in prison long after their continued incarceration has lost its value as being 'in the interest of justice' – sometimes until death.

Being Better

by Terry Robinson

Cruel. Heartless. Malicious and cold. That's how the prosecutor described me to a jury during his pitch for a verdict of death. He argued that I was, "...just mean and unfit to live." In the end, the jury agreed.

Four months after my arrival on Death Row, I stole money from an officer. Though inadvertent, it was theft, nonetheless. It happened one morning during weekly 'draw', while one officer was training another. At that time, available funds withdrawn from inmate accounts were counted and stapled together.

The new guy – or Newbie – handed me a stack of bills in fives and ones meant to total forty dollars. With no prior incidents or errors, I tucked the bills in my pocket and walked away. Within moments, a commotion stirred as one inmate started shouting over missing funds. Others became disgruntled and offered up chide remarks about the unfairness of the system. The senior officer tried to de-escalate the ruckus, while the new guy searched frantically through the money bag. I sympathized with the perplexity strewn on Newbie's face. It was his first day on the job.

After reassuring compensation, both officers exited the pod, as the ire amongst protesting inmates increased. With a prickly notion to count the money, I collected the bills from my pocket and discovered it wasn't one stack, but two. The staples in each stack had snagged one another and pieced the money together. I called over the guy to which the funds belonged, explained the mix-up and offered him the money.

"Keep it," he said, "Let the State pay for it, since they're trying to kill us, anyway." Tempers flared over systemic oppression, as the other inmates egged each other on. Reluctantly, I passed the money off to a friend – I was striking a blow to 'the State'.

Not only was the meager blow ineffective to the State, it was utterly deflected. I later found out the replacement funds were deducted from Newbie's salary. What a terrible feeling to know I was responsible for a mark on his work record. And by involving another party, I couldn't return the money, though keeping it cost me peace of mind.

Over the years, Newbie has gone on to become a well-respected officer. With an 18-year tenure of working on Death Row, he has seniority over all other staff. He's shown cordialness and consideration when enforcing policy, while effectively performing his duties. A kind, hardworking man, who seldom speaks, but is eager to flash a grin. As I've come to admire his professionalism, I'm reminded of my offense. Such a fine person deserves better from me – I deserve better from myself.

Recently, I was among several Death Row inmates selected for a random urinalysis. I arrived to find Newbie overseeing the process, as he went about his task with a grin. I'd often experienced discomfort whenever he was present – a nagging guilt that pecked at my conscience and impeded the wholeness of reform. Tonight's discomfort was more salient and intense, as I struggled with the idea of possible outcomes. What if Newbie had lost his job, or been accused of theft and criminally charged? I squeezed my eyes tightly as my inner voice gathered. Newbie deserved better. So did I.

Some idle chat was used to generate dialogue on self-reform. Then, with no one else around, my words spilled forth, "Yeah, man... many of us want to be better, but to do better, we have to own our truths. Just like the time when that forty-dollar draw come up missing…" At that point, I had Newbie's undivided attention. While confessing my role in the missing funds, I felt embarrassed, but liberated. I searched his eyes for a hint of anger. They stayed steady and unrevealing. I expressed my sincerity to return the funds and the difficulty of having involved another. His fixed look filled me with shame – a shame I well deserved.

Finally, Newbie settled his thoughts and said, "Thank you for telling me that." For eighteen years Newbie had been puzzled by the events of that day. He was certain about the money count and grateful to finally know what happened. I was moved to witness such genuine forgiveness, given instantly and without effort. I expected reprimand for my wrong-doing, instead, Newbie seemed relieved. His forgiveness was validation in the courage to right our wrongs. It was more than I deserved – it was a lesson in the goodness of humanity.

Potholes

by Joshua Kenyon

I wish there was a positive way to clear people's distorted perceptions – without making enemies of them. I wish there was a way people could realize their own flaws and laugh at them, while inspiring change. Some roads just *are* bumpier than others, and some of us keep hitting the same bump over and over. And then, sometimes, we adjust our actions to prevent us from being on that same road and hitting that same bump – no job, no home, divorce, prison, whatever the personal 'pothole' seems to be.

I'm doing the best I can, given the circumstances. I'm a 'master handler' in the Prison Trained Canine Companion Program. I just completed an Entrepreneurial Operations course and got accepted to Phi Theta Kappa Honor Society.

Often the advice given is that which is best taken, and I'm following my best advice. I'm becoming who I want to be.

I Hope

by Ashleigh Dye

Hope inside prison is a rare thing. You can always tell which people have it and which don't. The inmates who don't possess this precious gift are aimless. They roam, trying to find the next meaningless activity to fill time. They have a void that needs filling, and anything will do: drugs, sex, cards, fighting. They'll do whatever it takes to not think about the circumstances of their life. I know this because I used to be that person. I never engaged in fighting or drug use, so it was even easier for me to ignore what I was doing and justify my behavior as a product of me being so young. In truth, I was searching. I was hurting. I was guilty and ashamed. I was overwhelmed by the pain of a 48-year-sentence. I was disgusted by what I'd done to find myself in prison. Back then I didn't have the skills I needed to verbalize this to anyone. Nor was I even aware that I had a problem. All I knew was what I knew, and in reality, that was nothing. Until one day I encountered the *other* group of people.

The inmates who had hope were a different breed than I had seen. Something was strange about them, and I was drawn to them. They were alive. They carried themselves in a way I wanted to. Their heads were held high, and the guards spoke to them with respect. To me they looked like they had it together. I didn't realize at the time that what they had was hope. It just seemed like they cared a little more about what they did.

It was at this time I began taking college classes and moved into the college wing inside the prison.

I suddenly found myself surrounded – by hope. It filled the eyes of the ladies I lived with. They had dreams, plans, and purpose. It was infectious. They all had jobs and told me I needed one too. Nobody had ever told me I needed to get a job inside of prison. I thought all we did was play cards and sleep. I wanted what they had, so I got a job as a tutor. I was now working and going to class and spent my free time studying. I felt myself changing. It wasn't an overnight process, but I knew I was experiencing a transformation. Maybe I really could be like these other inmates, these adults who seemed so successful.

Unfortunately, I still didn't have a *purpose* in life. I didn't know *why* I was doing all of these things. *What* was going to keep me going? In 2017, I graduated with an Associate's Degree and became a certified optician. I even gave the valedictorian speech, and I got a job working for the Chaplain. Certainly, I was now just as successful as those women I sought to be like.

Just as I thought my life was coming together, it came crashing down. I got into a fight, and my actions landed me in segregation. I wasn't there long – just 10 days, but to me it was forever. As I walked back to the hole with hands cuffed behind me and head hung low, a guard said something to me.

"Aren't you the girl who works for the Chaplain?" he asked me with condemnation in his voice. All of the shame and guilt I felt before came flooding back to me. It was like I was the preacher's kid who got locked up. During my seg stay, those words played over and over again in my head. I had disappointed so many people. I prayed. It was all I knew how to do. I begged God for another chance. I asked Him to save me, and I thanked him – and I cried and cried and cried. Then I felt His love. It filled me up, and I knew that this was what it felt like to be Saved. I became a Christian in the lowest place I could find myself.

When I got out of isolation, the Chaplain showed me forgiveness and let me keep my job. I had to work hard to earn the respect back that I had built for years. I was determined now. I had found hope in that empty cell. I knew that no matter what, God would love me. I now had a goal post, something to hold on to no matter what happened. I was different, and people started to notice. I began self-evaluations and examining why my crime happened. I began working on becoming whole. I purposed myself to help others. I wrote proposals for classes. I started working with the Prison Dog Program. I wanted to give my hope to everyone.

Then, in 2019, I lost my brother to an overdose. He was my best friend, but we had been estranged since I became incarcerated. I never had the chance to make amends with him and that still haunts me. I think about myself in that moment, and what I would've done if I didn't have hope. But I did have it. I took that hope and organized a recovery summit for the prison. It was days of testimonies, powerpoints, and overdose awareness.

I hope I changed at least one woman's life in that time. Two years ago, Virginia passed a bill for people who committed their crimes as juveniles. After serving 20 years they will be eligible for parole. I was seventeen when I committed the heinous crime that took my mother's life. This new development, compounded with the hope I had, lit a fire inside me. I can see my future even more, and it is good. It is full of change, growth, and success. I hope I can use my life to change the lives of the people who hear my story. So I write. I write to impart hope to those who have none. I write to tell the stories I see. I write to share my muse with the world.

Mostly though, I hope...

I Was Seventeen – I'm Not A Violent Offender

by Louis Singleton, Jr.

After being in this prison system more years than I have lived on the streets, I'm feeling things I've never felt before – like my life was a waste. The world is almost thirty years ahead of me. When I think of people, I think of what life was like outside this prison in 1994. I still see the people who were once my school mates as kids. I still feel like a kid. I was one when I came here. I don't still think like a kid, but I still shoot basketball and exercise just like when I left the world. I am 44.

I've spent over half my life thinking about the events that led up to the night of January 11, 1994 – the day before my eighteenth birthday. Mobile is different now. If I lived there now, it never would have happened. There is a Coalition Against Bullying now. They have Anti-Bullying Awareness Weeks. There is something called a 'Bullyblocker'. You text a number if you are being bullied – your text goes straight to the District Attorney's office. I guess it's too late for me to text that. I did contact the right people at that time though. I went to my parents, the school, and the police. It's all on record. I just didn't have that Bullyblocker number. I would have used it if I had – and I wouldn't be here.

What makes me different than a kid that lives in Mobile today? I was bullied by men that didn't even go to my high school. There is no doubt the things that were done to me would have gotten a response if I had texted a hotline. It exceeded bullying. I was pushed around, chased, stalked – I was in high school and shot at on more than one occasion. If none of that had happened, what happened on January 11, 1994, wouldn't have happened. People make excuses for themselves all the time. That's not what this is. That's just reality. If the people who were supposed to had resolved the issue like they were supposed to, I, Louis Singleton, Jr., would never have done what I did. I wasn't raised to hurt anyone. That's not who I was or am.

I'm smarter though. I refuse to give into the criminal life. I get on to young brothers who can't seem to give up the drug life – until I break it down for them. They have big dreams of being Big Time Drug Dealers. They call me Unk. I try to encourage them to get out and do better for themselves. The at-home training my late mother gave me is embedded heavily in me. Knowing the difference between right and wrong will always be in me, no matter where they send me.

I'm living in the Alabama prison system, one of, if not the, worst prison system in America. Respect is at an all time low, but I never disrespect anyone, never have, never will. My mom taught me better. I hope those that were affected by my actions forgive me. I don't expect them to understand because, truly, you'd have to walk in my shoes. You'd have to be the seventeen year old kid who was getting shot at. I don't want that for anybody.

They see me as a 'violent offender'. I'm not violent. That label doesn't make me violent. I was seventeen, and it was a violent crime that never would have happened if I had been able to text that magic number and get help. I'm not even allowed to talk at my own parole hearing. They don't see me. They see 'violent offender'.

My first coach told me to never give up, no matter how badly you are losing the game. I haven't forgotten that to this day. It's the fourth quarter, the score is 44-10, the other team has the ball with 3:54 left on the clock. Play hard until the clock says 0:00. One time I was in a game playing defensive back, and a guy beat me on a broken coverage. He was running to the end zone, and I was chasing him. He got so far in front of me, I stopped pursuing him. He scored. I got chewed out heavily for that. Anything could have happened. He could have dropped the ball. From that day on, I've never given up.

Make My Hands Stronger!

by Charles Mamou, Jr.

People tell me to have faith, and I get it, I really do. I always want to have faith, but sometimes my mind is cluttered with so much doubt. They'll try to encourage me and say things like, "You are so strong, Chucky," meaning mentally. If only I had a penny for every time somebody told me that.

The truth is, they don't see it, but sometimes things hit me out of the blue, and I cry for reasons I'm not totally sure of. I stress about everything, from small to big issues. I recently became a grandfather. I can't tell you how it feels not being there for him. I failed as a parent to my own children. I see my grandson as my parental redemption ticket – however, I'm still locked up. And my stress continues.

Psychologically, there is nothing like being on Texas death row. Every day is a struggle within a struggle. You have to fight. You have to fight for toilet paper. You have to fight for commissary, a phone call, mail or Jpays, decent and edible food. And you have to keep on fighting just to be treated like a person and not some animal. What is even more insane is, just when you think you have resolved an issue, the next day you have to resolve it all over again. I think I've heard it said, "Hell is a repetitious place."

I rarely talk about the things that go on here. I don't talk about it to my loved ones, 'cause I don't want to worry them. If I knew they were worried, it would cause me more stress. So, I deal with it alone, as I have always done. Self-absorbed to self-abuse... self. I wouldn't recommend that mind-set to anyone. It's not ideal or healthy. But, in here, I know there is nothing any other human being can do to alleviate the inner loneliness.

Nehemiah once prayed to God, "Now strengthen my hands." He had to fight every day and when he grew weary, and it seemed he could not go on, he prayed to God for the strength to endure. So do I. That's how I get by. With God, I am able to get through this. Without God, I don't believe I'd be alive to be able to write these words with the hands that God has made stronger.

Savage Illusion

by Delaine Jones

I used to extort people in prison for money. Not
the soft or the weak, I was more of a bully's bully.
Prison can be like the N.B.A. – the guy who sits on
the end of the bench is better at this than *anyone*
you've *ever* known.   He's *earned* his spot on the
team.

I'd see a look in my victim's eyes, the silent
conversation most people turn their heads to avoid
having with those less fortunate than they are.
They saw me as the proverbial thug. A brute.

Simple minded. Someone peaking at the bottom of life, much the way boxers and MMA fighters are viewed – violent because life after high school couldn't be hash-tagged and the words needed to file articles of incorporation were too big to sound out.

I was someone society needed bars to separate itself from. I was one of those who'd *never* get it, who had chosen a pistol over a pen as the problem-solving tool of choice. Though it hurts to admit – it was true. That was me.

For the longest time, I could only be seen through my writing, and until I began to push this pen into the light, I spent my life dodging everyone's gaze. Caught without my pen and out in the open, I'd regurgitate snatches of things I'd heard, cutting and pasting quips into the proper spaces in conversations, twisting my face into the appropriate expressions, only to then slowly recoil from sight in the safety of silently vulturizing the words, thoughts, and comprehension of others. No one would know I was stupid, that I had serious issues simply reading the English language, that I was a fake and a thief of other people's skills and experiences. Why would I ever allow anyone to see that in me? So, like a child, I'd flash, I'd rage, I'd lash out to draw eyes elsewhere. Savage Illusion.

In high school I could dunk a basketball, but I couldn't read. I had to sound out words as I'd learned to do from Sesame Street as a kid. Never having owned a dictionary or even seen one in my family, I was able to understand a few words and reason out the jist of what was being said. It was like trying to decode a message written in a long dead Russian language. It made me feel small and hopeless. I felt that the world had somehow regressed into an antebellum-ish landscape, I an escaped slave, yearning for the freedom the secret of which was hidden in a language everyone else could speak, one I wasn't smart enough to master. I'd gaze wistfully at TV shows where parents played music for their unborn, read their babies bedtime stories or used hooked on phonics to teach their two-year-olds to read at a level higher than my own.

I imagine my teachers must've known, they must have noticed the string of clichés, quotes and song lyrics I would line together to answer questions and escape conversations, to appear what I thought to be 'smart' and not be rejected. Surely, teachers noticed the chair that I threw through a glass door in 7th grade. The teacher was demanding I read aloud in class. Look at the violence – not me! It cost my g-mom $100 we didn't have and me a week of school and a beating with an extension cord, a price I gladly paid.

Maybe it was because I was a multi-sport star athlete in a results-driven society that the lack of substance to my shine was deemed 'good enough'. After all, according to one history teacher, I'd be 'dead within five years of this conversation'. I was advanced to the 10th grade, and it became someone else's turn to fear-teach me history.

Yes, I was *that* kid. The one who'd fight you for joking that I was stupid, going from zero to sixty in a snap. Hearing what a friend never said. Being embarrassed by laughter that rattled like a tommy gun's 45's into my soul. Laughter only I could hear. Can a gangster doubt, feel alone?

It was my father, the preacher, who noticed during my weekly phone call from prison. Ever the pragmatic intellect who too often believes love isn't real unless it bruises, he said to me, "You're speaking in clichés, and you're spitting back the thoughts of others, DeLaine. You have your own mind! Stop being so damn lazy and use it!"

It was in segregation – 23 hours a day lockdown and isolation – I taught myself to read. With my spirit feeding on itself in a soup of depression, I learned to escape. It took all of thirty-two years for me to submit my first piece for publication though. Something I was forced to do, really. You see, when I'd tell people I was a writer, they'd ask if I was published. Can't be a writer unless someone else says you're worthy.

Dismiss, change the subject. Move along, little wannabe... man? Worthy? Extorting the extortionist?

When I received the first response from Walk In Those Shoes with a copy of the piece they'd published, I lost it! I danced like a fool, and cried like a snitch in a gangster's convention. It was as if Beyonce and Cardi B had taken my virginity at the same time!

Every person is responsible for their own self-worth, but to have the validation of others for something that has meant so much to me? All I can say is – *can you see me now?!*

My Life's GPS

by Charles Butcher

I lost my way sometime after 2006. I'm a Marine Corp veteran and father of four amazing children, as well as two beautiful grandchildren, but I still lost my way. I felt like I was on a train, headed down a mountain, without breaks, not realizing pride and selfishness were pushing the train faster, not to mention greed, alcohol and drugs. I thought I was in total control though. My train took me to prison for the first time in 2014.

Before that happened, I had tried to convince myself the people who meant the most to me didn't notice the condition of my train as it passed them every day. I told myself, *'I got this.'* I'd pay half the rent one week intending to pay the rest the next week and justifying it all with, *'Well, at least I paid something.'* Next week would come, the utilities would be due and the other half of the rent, plus the three kids that looked up to me needed lunch money, and the refrigerator was empty. I was so 'in control', I didn't realize the fifty dollars I just spent on drugs was taking food out of their mouths.

Life kept picking up speed. My GPS stopped working, and I was headed in a direction I never saw coming. I've tried, over the years, to figure out what made me lose focus on what was really going on. What I finally figured out was – it was me. I was the conductor. I derailed myself at the age of 48-years-old. I have no one to blame but me. And I needed help. I found help in God.

And I had to start believing I was worth happiness, love and forgiveness. I also figured out I had nothing to lose and everything to gain. Looking back, I think prison may have saved my life. I could have died on my path. I think it was a sign from above, telling me to steer in the direction of freedom, family and forgiveness. The most important change I've ever made is letting God take over as my conductor.

Corresponding Connection

by Geoff Martin

I never knew my father. I have long since come to terms with that, but as a young child, it crushed me. I questioned why my dad would not want to be '*my*' dad and eventually concluded he just didn't love me. Years later, when my own daughter was born, I held her in the delivery room and made a promise to both of us that I would never fail her the way my father failed me – never cause her to question my love. I broke that promise spectacularly when she was only four years old. I went to jail and, later, prison with a life sentence.

My broken promise put my daughter in a highly vulnerable demographic. One in forty children in this country is affected by parental incarceration, the math works out to 2.6 million kids with at least one parent in a cage. This separation afflicts children with emotional and behavioral problems, low grades in school, high dropout rates, and a higher risk of incarceration. These effects scream the importance of incarcerated parents staying connected to their kids and their lives as much as possible. But how do you do that from here?

I discovered my answer while wasting away in county jail for two years. I spent most of the time sifting through the wreckage of my former life and weighing the damage my actions caused. One of the most tormenting pieces of debris was the lost connection to my daughter. In desperation, I did the only thing available – I wrote letters to her, pouring my heart out to the little girl left behind.

There were tears as I expressed sorrow for not being the father I had promised and knowing she would suffer for my mistakes; there were smiles (even laughs) as I shared some of our good memories – endless Disney movies, ad-lib bedtime stories, and epic hide-and-seek games in our home, where the actual challenge was not finding the uncontrollable giggler hiding in front of the sofa.

As the letters piled up, a family member reached out offering to receive them and, when my daughter was older, give them to her if she ever asked about me. With great difficulty, I managed to stifle my excitement. I did, however, allow a glimmer of hope in my heart that we might one day reunite.

There are prison programs that assist incarcerated fathers with connecting to their kids – Fatherhood Accountability, One Day With God, etc. These are commendable programs worth taking advantage of, but they are mere drops in the bucket. It takes so much more to develop strong, loving relationships with our children. I found that writing letters helped me. Through letters our children get to know who we are. Through writing letters, we also get to process the separation as well. Some may hesitate for fear of sounding foolish, and I struggled with this at times. But I fought through with the belief that any emotion infused in a letter will be felt when it is read. What I wrote on those pages, the good and the bad, eventually made me real to my daughter, all of my tears and smiles made an impact.

I received my daughter's first letter seventeen years into my sentence. The very first line – the first thing she wanted to say to me after so much time – *"Hey, dad, I just finished your letters and would like for us to get to know each other... again."*

I Find Serendipitous Strength in Others

by Charles Mamou, Jr.

I had a plethora of 'special visits' within the past week – four visitation days filled with two different people, for a total of sixteen hours. Had I not been awarded such visits from caring friends, I would have spent those hours within a defeat filled prison cell.

During those four hours of conversation, topics range from favorite TV shows – they liked Mork &

Mindy, I liked Punky Brewster – to cartoons like the Smurfs, Care Bears, Voltron, and Underdog – a classic.

We talk about food, although my guests are all vegans. They talk about nuts and crackers, while I ask, "Where's the beef?" When they buy me snacks, they refuse to eat in front of me. No one likes getting food stuck in their teeth around me – what's up with that?

We discuss politics, books read, family issues and jobs. We talk about their dealings just as much as mine, and we will cover a wide range of wild and mundane topics. At some point the unavoidable will arise, though I try to avoid it – my pending execution/murder. After all, it's the reason we are 'here'. It's why our sailing ships crossed paths within the massive sea of interactions.

My friend, Mary, is from England where they drive on the wrong side of the road, though she begs to differ. It's where they say 'arse' instead of ass. Can you imagine Cardi B singing about her 'arse'? Just

don't sound right. Mary comes from a land where
Mary Poppins isn't a myth – rather a legend.
When she told her family and friends that she was
coming to America to visit a man on Texas death
row they asked, "Have you gone mad (lost your
mind)?"

People often ask me if I am mad. Bitter. I'm not
pretentious by nature, and what you see is exactly
what you get. So – in the tone of my cussing
pastor and actor, Samuel L. Jackson, "You damn
right I get mad and bitter!" Even though hardly
anyone ever sees that in me.

"Chucky, I have one more question. I would like to
know just as the people of England would like to
know – how do you stay so strong? How can you
stay smiling and positive?"

It's a fair question. One I'm often asked. And,
bravado has it's place – but not in my story. To
put on a brave face would make a mockery of the
struggle of being isolated all day for decades
without the touch of another human being's skin.

It is written, 'It is not good for man to be alone.' I guess my oppressors didn't get that memo. How do I stay strong? I pointed to her through the glass, to her surprise. "Me?"

"You and people like you."

It's not lost on me that it's not easy entering a prison to come visit me. I understand the money and time so freely given to afford me a few hours of comfort. I'm always grateful for it. We are all – literally – strangers from different cultures, with different likes and different social economic norms. The thought that strangers come to my aid and show me what love is – is humbling. Without my friends, I would be nothing... Nothing.

I draw strength from the acts of others who display a courage and unmanacled devotion on a scale that I can never fully comprehend. I think about how busy their lives are and how they still find the time to think about me and write to me. They visit me knowing they are going to be made uncomfortable by guards.

I think about my friend, Debbie, who was diagnosed with brain cancer and lung cancer and has undergone multiple surgeries within the past year. She has been a constant in my life since 2004. And when she was told I lost my final appeal she argued with the doctor to discharge her so she could fly to see me and offer comfort so I wouldn't feel alone.

I think about my play-daughter and her mom and how they have enriched my life by adopting me into their family. They are two of the greatest humanitarians my eyes have ever witnessed – and they shed tears for me and the injustice that has befallen me for two decades. Some people have seen Gandhi, Mandela, Sojourner Truth, Dr. King and so on – to them, they are heroes. My play-daughter and her mother are my icons, my heroes – my angels. If I don't live to see another day, I know I have been cared for by people that are greater than this life.

Then there's Mary. She's laughter. She's Lucille Ball funny and one of the most non-judgmental people there is. She's a great religious orator and an advocate for children who have been abused or suffer mental illness. She is a fascinating person and a genuine friend, as well as her husband.

These people are the core of my support group and the source of the strength others see in me. If I'm strong, it's because I have been shown and taught what strength looks like and feels like. I am strong because I have been loved freely by those who so freely love. That's strength.

Influence

by John Johnson

Coming from the Southwest side of Detroit, opportunities were very poor, the bad ones outnumbering the good ones almost ten to one, with little likelihood of being successful or legit. I lost three relatives to gun-violence in one summer alone. Most of the friends I grew up with are either dead, on drugs, or in jail.

I'm older now. I spend most of my time studying and manifesting connections that support self-help and development. My agenda now is to make a difference. I understand what happened to us, and where we went wrong and what it takes to avoid a place like 'this', where the system is broken and built to further break you. Contrary to rehabilitating, it encourages criminality.

I once heard, "If you want to hide something from a negro, put it in a book..." Is there truth to this? I had to pick up a book or two to see what I had been missing all those years, things I didn't understand that I let slide by without answers. One thing I learned is that the things a child sees, hears, and experiences throughout childhood, will most likely have a profound effect on that kid once they reach adulthood. The first traumatic memory I have is of me as a five-year-old standing in the middle of a stairwell watching my dad as he lay on our living room floor in a pool of his own blood due to gun violence. Later, at the age of ten I watched a young man shoot and kill his uncle in broad daylight.

Whether it was gun-violence I saw, domestic violence, sexual abuse or the drug infestation that overwhelmed my environment, it neither begins nor ends with 'me'. This is an environmental disease that infects the minds and spirits of children in general – not just mine. Negative influence is a highly contagious virus and is able to transmute anything pure into poison.

Knowing the things I know today, makes it my responsibility to help the kids, the most vulnerable to the negativity and the ones who will grow to pass the illness from one individual to the next. It is my responsibility to help them make better decisions and provide them with solutions that discourage violence and trauma, and encourage love and longevity.

My son just turned thirteen years old. After being absent in his life for ten years, one of the first things he spoke to me about was needing help surviving his future. I needed guidance and help as a kid and now – they need me. They need *us*.

Thought Is My Existence

by Jerrod Buford

As I entered the county jail, a C.O. in intake recognized me as a local tattoo artist. Mine was a high profile case, and I was segregated from inmates with lesser charges. Holding back emotions and the regret that came with the initial realization of what I had done, where I was and all those I had failed, I steeled myself in an effort to make resolve with my guilt and ultimately grow.

Within 24 hours, I was moved to the top floor of the jail where inmates with mainly violent crimes were housed. The pod was on lockdown for a fight. My name was called as I walked to my newly assigned living quarters. "Who dat?" I responded, recognizing the voice as a client of mine from tattoo parties I had done in his neighborhood.

My cell door opened, and I entered. Single-man cell. I cried. Looking at myself in the warped mirror, I decided then that I would come out better than I was in that moment. I was unstable mentally, angry at life, financially uneducated and a flawed character, failing to accept accountability for my reality. I laid down, visualizing the moment of my crime and sorry for the pain I know I caused my two sons, my mother and my family.

I began writing poetry, expressing my regrets and acknowledging the pain I caused so many. So many! I hurt people who also have children, mothers and other family members. There is no reason good enough, no justification for what I did. I turned myself in because I felt the guilt that I did not expect to feel. The guilt and desire to make amends with those I hurt settled in my core like an anchor. How do I grow from this?

I listened to my victims at my preliminary hearing, speaking on what I did and expressing the trauma I caused them. I am a naturally empathetic person, so their pain resonated with me. I hurt people. I realized then that I must be who I am and accept myself with that truth. I don't enjoy, nor do I desire to hurt people.

At my sentencing, at which I took a plea deal, I apologized to my victims. I don't know if they felt my sincerity, my disgust with myself, or even my desire to be the best version of myself going forward. I am certain that none of those things really resonated with them for the sight of me must have brought to mind how my actions brought us to that point.

I was fortunate, I think, to be sent to the prison I am currently serving my sentence at. It's no different than any other prison in regard to the treatment by staff, violence, intoxicants and many other distractions on the path to rehabilitation, but there are many programs that have helped me in my evolution towards a better me.

This time is mine, and I know that I am fortunate for having a foundation of principles guiding me in self-improvement and growth for myself and my family and a future as a contributing member of society. My thoughts and desires are aligned, and my reality is more tangible because of what I have done with my time within the parameters of my freedom.

Knowledge and acceptance of my own self was the first step, acknowledging my wrong, acknowledging how deeply I hurt my victims, children, family and friends, and knowing what I can do from within these walls to accept and change my reality.

This knowledge made me accept accountability and responsibility for my emotions and character development. I utilize the library to obtain a healthier understanding of all things pertaining to my growth. I have assumed healthier habits and practices in my daily life and deal with freedom in realistic degrees and expectations. I no longer accept powerlesseness over self and have developed the ability to see the value in all things and people, major and minor.

Today I am better than I have ever been because my intentions and actions are clear. I choose to add value to all I encounter in an effort to bring forth a greater good. I know the true test is out in society, and I look forward to the day I am afforded that degree of freedom. I continue and will continue to do those things I know have the beneficial quality of contributing to the greater good.

I now think outside this box and have created books, art, youth programs and other endeavors. And I write this to inspire others in the same situation to change your perception of where you are and what you can do – and what your time means to you.

T.hought **I.**s **M.**y **E.**xistence.

"The best time to plant a tree is 20 years ago, the next best time is now."

Chinese Proverb

Regardless of Our Flaws

by Joshua Kenyon

Dear Sugar Baby,

Sometimes the lines get blurred, and I don't know which of us is saving the other. I have no idea what you've been through, where you've been, or where you are going, but when I met you, I knew it was my job to do the best I could for you. What you don't know is, while I'm teaching you the skills to succeed, you are doing the same for me.

Thank you for having the patience to teach me patience and for never complaining, even though we all have bad days. Thank you for showing me that regardless of our flaws we can love and be loved. I've been known to put my life on the edge, self-destruction the product of my decisions, but I cannot allow that while your precious life is in my hands.

You've never cared about my past, what I look like or what I have. You just look at me with those beautiful green eyes, your tail waggin', simply happy with the moments we share together in our 6' x 9' home.

Thank you for training me Sugar Baby. I'll miss you.

Josh

I am one of many trainers, and Sugar Baby is one of many dogs. The Colorado Prison Trained K-9 Companion Program has given many individuals the opportunity to see the change they can create.

Just like us, some of these dogs have been hurt, abandoned, and lack the knowledge they need to succeed. Also like us, some of them are on their last chance. We invest ourselves, 24 hours a day, to provide them with the socialization skills, obedience training and love they need.

To take a scared, hurt, or distrustful being and teach them to become a fun-loving and playful part of someone's family, sometimes in weeks, shows us what we are capable of. The dogs we get to care for are amazing and they teach us how amazing we are along the way. If they can turn out so wonderful, then we can too.

My Two-Voiced Muse

by Timothy Johnson

Eighteen years ago I killed two men during an altercation while tailgating at an NC State football game. I cannot restore their lives, but I can live each day in a way that honors them both, that honors the sorrow their loved ones endure each day, and that honors the burden my family has been forced to carry. By living with the values of compassion, honesty, integrity, and social responsibility, my life can serve to restore brokenness rather than cause it.

Surrounded by the gray concrete walls of a jail cell, I was lost in a pit of despair – despair from the guilt of taking two lives, from forever changing everything for at least three families, from thinking my life was nothing but a disaster. The despair left me struggling to find even a glimmer of hope. Ruinous thoughts swirled – *'I have destroyed everything.' 'My life means nothing.' 'It would be better if I had never been born.'* Yet, that abyss was not my grave. The words of two mothers – mine and one of my victims – have served as my muse, lifting me out of the pit of despair and inspiring me to live with purpose.

My mother leaned forward, wanting only to wrap her arms around me, but the dingy, scratched Plexiglass made contact impossible. The day after I was arrested and charged with two counts of murder was a visitation day at the Wake County jail. I crumpled against the cubicle's side, unable to look into her tear-teeming eyes. *How could I have let her down so terribly when she had sacrificed so much?* Her words broke through the desire to fade into non-existence. "Look at me. Timothy, look at me." My chin trembled as my watery eyes were forced to meet her gaze. My mother's words then cast a lifeline to my drowning soul. "I love you. I love you, and I will never give up on you." When I thought I was too far gone to save, her love rescued me.

A number of people testified during the sentencing phase of my trial; the words of one mother have echoed in my head since the moment she spoke them. Her son was a Marine on the verge of leading his platoon to Iraq and a graduate of the U.S. Naval Academy in Annapolis. His mother shared how proud she was of him, of the man he was becoming even more than his accomplishments. Then, she acknowledged one of her regrets. "I will never again answer the phone to hear his military staccato voice, saying, 'Hello, Mother'." Her imitation of his cadence and greeting demonstrated her deep and painful sorrow with utmost precision, piercing my heart to its core, revealing the anguish my actions caused the mothers of these men.

Only two things can compel a person to truly change – something incredibly good or horribly bad. The merging voices of my muse grants me both. My mother's words remind me of the blessings still in my life – the love and support of my family, the prospect of another heart's day alive, the opportunity to positively impact the people and world around me. *Les Miserables* author, Victor Hugo, declared, "The greatest happiness of life is the conviction that we are loved; loved for ourselves, or rather, loved in spite of ourselves." In spite of myself, in spite of disastrous mistakes, my mother communicated love and value when I was on the brink. She imparted the belief that my life could still have value. The words of that mother remind me of what I took and therefore the steep consequences of compromising on life-values. Her words motivate me to maintain course on making positive choices guided by values instead of the selfish choices that shattered lives and dreams.

When guilt and shame stir up the roiling sea of despair, when this riptide sucks me under and pulls me away from the shore, spinning and twisting, turning and rolling me, over and over, until I cannot determine which way is up or down, my two-voiced muse reveals the glimmering hope of living with compassion and social responsibility. Their words dispel the disorientation and pull me to the surface. My muse reminds me to look beyond myself, beyond circumstances, and encourage others.

There are things men, especially men in prison, do not talk about. We do not talk about pain or loneliness. We do not talk about despair. We say we are fine, when we are anything but fine. We put on an outside mask of strength, because to display weakness brings vulnerability. When we are struggling with despair, we feel utterly alone, like nobody knows our pain, our loneliness, our hopelessness. Yet we are not as alone as we think.

In fact, we are not alone at all. Many of us struggle with despair but never talk about it. A person struggling with despair needs to know they are not alone, that there is hope. Someone must start the conversation.

My muse gave me the courage to start that conversation, to face the vulnerability of admitting I know the depths of despair, the practice of putting on a mask all day, saying I am fine when I am dying on the inside. I know the performance of smiling and laughing around others, but ending the day by walking in my cell, shutting the door, sliding down the wall, and sitting on the concrete slab floor, arms around my knees, head on my forearms, drained of all energy from the performance of "fine, just fine."

By sharing my struggle, others can know they are not alone or lost in despair. They do not have to hide their pain or put on a mask. There is hope. Their lives have value and purpose. I can be for them what my muse has been for me – a source of inspiration and motivation to rise from the depths of the circumstances of my creation and sail the shimmering sea of a life of purpose.

Young Thoughts Caused It All

by Ricardo Ferrell

I constantly ask the relatively preserved looking 62-year-old man in the mirror, *"How in the hell did you let me get caught up in this madness?"* I can't help but reflect on the 15-year-old boy who thought he could navigate the mean streets of Detroit and live and survive on his own. Little did he know his backward and irresponsible thinking would lead him toward a world of trouble. The man staring sternly back at me in that rusted, steel framed plastic mirror constantly reminds me of the boy whose bad choices and poor decisions caused a litany of problems...

Without addressing the neglect, abuse and trauma you experienced when you were just a little fella, those experiences build up and contributed to you exploring and resorting to an unhealthy outlet that lead to criminality and a propensity for violence. Some 47 years ago, your young thoughts influenced and ruled everything about you. Jewels, you had so much going for you, and you threw it all away for what amounts to insignificant, temporary gratification.

Man, do you remember when you were hired as a files clerk for the Genesee County Department of Social Services and were one of the only male employees in an office full of women? You were being vetted at 17 years old to become a permanent employee with the Michigan Department of Social Services to work as a staff member at W.J. Maxey Boy's Training School.

You always excelled in your endeavors, stood out amongst most of your peers. In grade school many of your fellow students displayed jealousy because you were always getting A's and B's and winning spelling bees. Had you stayed on track and not dropped out of school, no telling where you would be right now. I know you could've been anything you put your mind to – a doctor, a lawyer, judge, scientist, even an astronaut, but you were drawn to what you thought was the fascinating street life. A life that ultimately caused you to lose your freedom. I know you're probably saying, "Why didn't you pull up on me back then and give me some game because maybe I would've taken a different path."

I can't turn back the unstoppable hands of time, they wait on no one. If I had the chance to do it all over again, I would make sure you knew and learned the ropes to get through the life that unfolded before your young, innocent eyes. If given the chance, I would lend you some advice...

*Make amends by trying to right the wrongs
you've done.
Learn to forgive yourself for those you've harmed.
Face your fears and insecurities without pause.
Be comfortable with being uncomfortable.
Rebuild the community you helped to destroy.
Make something of your life and live righteously.
Love yourself and others.
Be compassionate, kind, loving, and patient.
Help as many people as you possibly can without
reward.
Do everything you can to make this world better.*

*You should know some good came out of who you
once were. You were beyond brilliant, and had
you embraced your God given greatness and
utilized your inner-most being, tapped into the
core of your existence, man, there's absolutely no
limits to where you could've soared in this
universe. I hope you will one day find it in your
heart to forgive me for leading you astray with
my wayward thinking, because from that foolish
thinking, an attitude of destruction formed, and it*

filtered into very dangerous and negative behavior that contributed to people getting hurt and you messing up your life. I am not going to blame the environment, the neglect, abuse, or trauma that we experienced, but I want you to understand one thing, all of this wasn't our fault. There were other factors beyond our control that made it hard for us to navigate in this world simply because of the color of our skin. Yeah, the deck has always been stacked against us, there have been systems strategically placed for us, as black men, to fail, and blindly destroy one another. But you and I have the spirits of our ancestors flowing in our soul and we will and shall overcome all the obstacles, struggles, trials and tribulations we may come to face.

They say everything happens for a reason, so I will venture to say it's no accident things turned out the way they did. On some real, 100 stuff, it all boils down to one's thoughts causing it all.

In Loving Memory

Being incarcerated means coping with grief in isolation.

Letter To An Angel

by Jarod Wesenberg

Tell me, Sis,

How we supposed to get past this?

I'll never be content

Talkin' about in the past tense.

And I gotta ask this...

Was it my fault?

Should I have kept it all in and masked it?

I mean... I called you Angel, but it was only

metaphorically!

I didn't mean for you to go and get a halo and wings!

Ups! Down! But we never meant to say those things!

I was only mad... and ignorant... I didn't know how to act!

I didn't know how to be – a brother.

I was too busy tryna be a 'G',

Something I wasn't!

But see, I don't wanna go get this tattoo saying R.I.P!

And I know how you felt about Ma and Kareem,

But did you miss 'em that much?

That you had to leave so early,

Just to feel they touch?

Damn, Sis! What about us? (what about *us*?)

What about Rob? What about T.J.?

He didn't even get enough... of you.

Was it all just too much... for you?

Backbone to a family?

Mother *and* father to a son,

Yet, you weren't manly!

And what about, Mama?
She raised her own four,
And here's another two.
Okay, more like three, we all know how Rob can
be!
And I don't mean to sound selfish,
But fuck that! What about *ME*?
Do I accept this? Take it in stride?
Or do I come with you?
To spend a little bit of time,
Standing in line?
'Cause you know everyone makes it to the gates,
But not everyone makes it inside.
So, when you make it in...
Vouch for me,
Let God know I'm not that bad!
Or at least ask for a weekend pass!
So when I'm in Hell, it won't feel like it.
The way I make the memories from those three
days last!
I just wanna come kick it with you and Beamer.
I know she there!
All dogs go to Heaven,

They're innocent creatures.

Now, back to the subject,

How do you want me to deal with this pain?

Guess I'm happy to have it,

'Cause if I would've went before you,

Lord only knows what that would've done to your
brain.

Brain? Well, there's some screws loose,

But I would give you mine in a heartbeat.

Now I wish I could just give you a heartbeat!

My heartbeat!

I'm feeling kinda dead inside,

There's a lot of lead inside.

I would sink if I went swimmin'.

I'd rather go feet first into the flames,

Then to have this feeling!

And what's the correct way to mourn an Angel?

I don't know!

But why the fuck did you have to be the one to
teach me!

You were the only one who could reach me,

The only one to feed me...

All that love that God blessed you with!

I'm sorry for all the shit I ever stressed you with.

Remember, *you* told me about Kareem?

And I was asking, 'Who goin' to be next and 'ish?

I *knew* it wouldn't be you!

You didn't even make the list.

I coulda never guessed this 'ish!

Yeah! Yeah!

I hear you now, tellin' me not to stress the 'ish,

But that's easier to say.

My puzzle been missing pieces,

and another one just went away...

Coping With Conviction

by Terry Robinson

He stormed on to Death Row with his fists balled tight, a sneer on his face that was either a challenge or a deterrent. His wavy hair was spinning, too well-kept to have just fought someone, so if he wasn't in trouble, then he must be looking for it. *'Who the hell comes through the doors on Death Row inviting conflict with hardened killers?'* I thought. Not me. I arrived on Death Row the day before, and I was trying to go unnoticed. He was trouble alright, with his tattooed neck and gangster lean as he slung his sack of property on the top bunk with a thud. Young. Unruly. Someone to avoid. My judgment of him was just getting started when, unexpectedly, he turned and offered me a cigarette.

That was how I first came to know Eric Queen, it was upon our arrival on Death Row. Two young men trying to wrap our heads around the most terrifying thing to happen to a person. At least, that's what receiving the death penalty was for me. Eric seemed too mad to give a damn, an anger that burned without direction. I should've been just as mad since I was there without cause. I'd taken a beating to my reputation at trial court with the lies and accusations. Maybe I thought playing nice would earn me a reprieve, when the truth was, I could have used some of Eric's anger.

We bonded over Newport cigarettes, shared adversity and the recent events that brought us to Death Row. As the menthol smoke spewed from our lungs and dissipated into nothingness, so too

did the intensity ease from Eric's face. What I
once thought was an unruly, trouble-making thug
was really a harmless-looking average guy.
Harmless with the potential to be lethal, like a
steel trap that lies rusting idly away over time as
long as nobody comes fucking with it. His brown
eyes gleamed with the curiosity of someone eager
to learn. His skin was the color of sunset at the
end of a blistering day. A man in his early
twenties, his youthful facial features were likely to
require proof of I.D., with a gap-tooth smile that
he sported with such confidence it left him on the
right side of handsome.

He said he preferred to be called E-Boogie. Funny.
He didn't seem like the dancing type. He bobbed
when he walked, his arm like a pendulum swaying
ridiculously side-to-side with each step, but that
appeared to be the extent of his rhythm. Still, it
occurred to me that almost every black person on
Death Row went by a nickname. Bedrock. Yard
Dog. Napalm. Dreadz. There was even an Insane.
I thought to get me one since the name 'Terry' was

in no way as intimidating as Insane. That was the night I became known as Eye-G and E-Boogie and I first shook hands.

In the days and weeks to come, E-Boogie and I grew to know more about each other. I considered my own story as boring as a silent film, but his was action-packed. He told me about being a military brat, though I must say it sounded more like a confession. The packing up and leaving friends, always the new guy at school, the unstableness of it all. I couldn't pretend to know the struggles of life on the base, so I mostly listened. Many of his tales lasted about as long as a punch line, then he was on to the next. It was only when he reached his experiences with gangs that he spoke at length. The only thing I knew about gangs was that I didn't want to know about gangs, but without it I could never fully come to know and understand E-Boogie.

Out of tolerating our differences, we found we had many things in common. We played basketball together every day, usually on the same team, but we both had a competitive spirit so rivalry was in the air. Our love for music kept us up at night listening to rap songs and debating which hiphop artist was better. Sometimes it was an all day affair at the poker table, cheating our asses off with hand signals only to walk away with a few pennies to show. We liked the same movies, ate the same foods and drank about the same amount of prison hooch before staggering to our bunks and crashing for the night. Every day spent with Eric was taxing, yet we woke up and did it all over again as our shenanigans kept the adverse conditions of Death Row at bay and staved off the awaiting pain.

Our coping with conviction did not come without dissent from the other inmates. Some thought that our rowdiness violated their personal space. It kind of did, but it wasn't intentional. Prison strips a person of almost every dignity, every liberty you could think of until all you have is an incredible sense of personal space. It's all bullshit when even our personal space belongs to the state, yet it's the only thing left for us to claim in this world in order to say we're still here. No one understood that more than me. Hell, I was holding on to something too. While they were griping about personal space, I was fighting to keep my sanity. Even E-Boogie and all his thug moodiness would not deliberately infringe on someone's personal space. Yeah... he was mad as hell at times, but I think it was more at himself. His and my antics were simply that – antics to distract from the chaos of having a death sentence. It was hard to accept the reality that my life as I knew it was over.

Nothing good lasts forever. That's the motto of Death Row. We'd gone a few months fending off the misery and picking each other's spirits up. Maybe we had no right to be enjoying ourselves while Death Row was grinding away at the minds of those around us. Well, E-Boogie and I would both learn that the misery was infallible and friendships were bound to suffer. It started one day with a dispute between he and I over something so petty I can't remember. The

exchange got heated. We both were talking shit.
Suddenly E-Boogie called me out to fight. We
argued over something so frivolous I believed he
wasn't serious. I walked up to him, looked him in
the eyes – and he punched me in the face. I was so
shocked, my breath caught in my chest and my
heart sunk with betrayal. Eric, the person I relied
on the most, had violated my personal space. The
fight that ensued wasn't much of a fight at all,
rather a bunch of grappling to try and salvage our
friendship. Before the day was over, we were back
in each other's good graces... but something
between us had changed.

Afterwards we explored other friendships while
maintaining a strained connection. We still got
together and did all the things we enjoyed, but
when it was over we'd go our separate ways. Eric
made friends with a few people whose company I
did not care for. Even from a distance, I could see
his mood darkening to a point where I was overly
concerned. He started getting into fights, in fact,
he and I would go another round. It wasn't

anything our friendship couldn't survive, but it wedged us further apart. One day we watched Eric's sister, Kanetra, play college basketball before the nation on TV. After the game he went to his cell and closed the door, proud and isolated for two days.

On a few occasions he and I got together and talked like old times. I hadn't realized how much I missed him. At the time, I wasn't doing all that great in coping with Death Row, but Eric seemed to be doing a lot worse. I promised myself I would be there for him more, the way he was there for me.

Eric opted out of the annual basketball tournament, which left everybody on Death Row like... *"What?"* He was a top player. He upped everybody's game. The tournament wouldn't be the same without him. He did, however, coach that year. I was chosen to play on his team and man – we butted heads all season. I didn't expect favoritism, I was too proud for that. I earned my spot on the team. In the end, we lost terribly in the elimination round, and I didn't speak to Eric for over a week. Now, I wish I had.

I was at the card table that day when the announcement came over the PA system.

"Lockdown. Lockdown. All inmates report to your assigned cell. Lockdown. Report to your cells now."

It was 5:00 p.m. We hadn't gone to dinner yet. What the hell was going on? We packed up the poker chips and headed to our rooms. My biggest concern was winning my money back. The chatter started behind the doors. Speculation mostly. A fight broke out downstairs. A fight? Downstairs? E-Boogie was housed downstairs. Money was now the furthest thing from my mind. I knew in my heart it was Eric. The cell doors stayed closed throughout the night, and I went to bed wondering with whom Eric had a fight.

The next morning, I was standing in front of the mirror brushing my teeth when a guy popped up at the door. His face was rather long, his eyes dodgy, and he shifted from one heel to the other. He said that he was just dropping by to check on me since he knew E-Boogie and I were close.

"What the hell you talkin' 'bout? What happened to E-Boogie?" I asked.

"He hung himself, dawg. E-Boogie is dead."

There were no tears to soothe the burning in my eyes as they were a river cascading down my heart. I wanted to sling my toothbrush aside, run downstairs and save him, but my chance for that was gone. I couldn't remember the last words I said to him, and I couldn't forget saying nothing. I felt like I failed him for not being there for him like he was for me when I needed a friend the most. The word about Eric spread like wild fire in a gasoline storm. He was found hanging in a mop room closet and pronounced dead on the scene. I realized Eric had been fighting after all; I just never guessed it was a fight with himself. Maybe

there wasn't much I could have done about that,
but I owed it to him to try.

Eric Queen perished on August 5, 2007. He was
28. He was a hothead at times, but he was
generous, and if he loved you, he made sure you
knew it. Eric made mistakes in his life, but I never
heard him make excuses. In fact, one time he said
to me, "Life don't bend over for nobody, Eye-G.
We just gotta roll with it."

I'm still wondering where he got that from with his
young ass. Eric swore he was a philosopher, and at
times he really was. Dude was smart as hell. He
could figure out anything – he just chose to figure
out the streets. Can't say I blame 'im. The streets
are tempting; they've led a lot of good people down
bad paths. Still, there is redeem-ability after the
streets. I wonder if Eric believed he could be
redeemed. We never talked particularly about the
crime that led him to Death Row, so no
speculation there. But I know he had regrets in
other areas of his life – we both did. It was us
sharing those stories and being vulnerable with

one another where we became like brothers. I just wish he knew his life was so much more than the evil that plagued him that day. If nothing else, his redeeming quality was in all that he did for me. I was spiraling into an unhealthy mental space when he walked through the doors that night. Eric put aside his own burdens to get me through my worst of times. I only wish I could've done the same for him... maybe through my writings I can still try.

The World?!

by Delaine Jones

*"We are all that we've got! If I don't do for you,
who else will? The world? They wouldn't piss
down your throat if your guts were on fire!"*

Those were words my normally silent maternal
grandmother lived by. I've oft sat in my cell and
wondered at the cruelty – the experiences – she
must have endured. What had been done to that
sweet southern girl to bring such a harsh reality?
And had those deeds matriculated into the truths
that colored my thoughts and actions, the reality of

my life thus far? If you are what you eat – how about what you're fed?

My grandmother didn't give birth to my uncles Benni and Squeaky (Victor and Richard, respectfully), but she raised, loved, fed, nursed, and fought for them, just as she did her own. They slept in the same beds, bathed in the same tubs, were hugged by the same arms, but I imagine it was tough for them. Their birth mom was a heroin addict who couldn't care for them but for her addiction. Their father was the father of five of my grandmother's eleven children.

Now, my Uncle Benni was slightly 'swish' in his gayness. He was called 'Benni' after the classic Sir Elton John song, *Bennie and the Jets.* Growing up, he was more apt to be found with his sisters doing each other's hair rather than running with his brothers. It was braids, barrettes, and clothes verses bats, balls and the hustle of the streets with brothers who clowned, taunted, jeered, and refused to show love.

I always loved my Unc. Yeah, he was gay, a bad thing from the way it was thrown in his face, but I didn't know what that was. All I knew was that he loved us and paid attention to us. I remember once seeing the flash of anger in his eyes upon realizing we hadn't been anywhere since the last time we saw him – five and a half months earlier.

He grabbed a newspaper and in a flurry of ironing, braiding, and cocoa butter, we were off on some adventure – the movies, a radio sponsored jam session in a far away park, the carnival, the swap meet. Hot lines, jojo fries, cold cream sodas!

I was still just a short stack when my lil' sister and I heard the knock at the front door at 2 a.m. one night. We were still young enough to share a bed. Then we heard the familiar voice that had us out of that bed in a flash! Looking in the window, my Uncle Benni told us to open the door. Seeing him through the window, we didn't bother to turn on the lights in our excitement, and when we opened the door, there was snow on the ground and the air was sharp. My grandmother sharply asked who we'd let in her house at that hour, and Unc answered to keep us out of trouble.

"It's just Benni, Mommy, I lost my key," he slurred by way of explanation.

We didn't care that he was drunk. He often came home that way. Benni's lifestyle saw him in a lot of bars and gay clubs. He was a performer. He used to dress up like Diana Ross and sing in shows. Us kids had found photos in the single bag that he kept in an upstairs closet as if it were his refusal to give up on a people who didn't really want him around – not the gay version.

So, he lived his life mostly apart from us. We had no idea where or how he lived, other than the shows, no idea who his friends or loves were. We just knew he could vogue and dance his ass off.

"If we don't do for each other, who else will?"

My sister and I took him by the hands and guided him up the stairs in the dark, where he changed into his floral muumuu and climbed into our bed. Just as he'd shown up without warning, Unc often left in the same fashion, so we always wanted to keep him close. The rank alcohol smell was a price we'd willingly pay just to keep the magic of him near.

But when the two of us climbed into bed next to his already sleeping form, it was wet! Was he so drunk he'd peed the bed?! Finally, we turned on the lights in the room and were greeted by the horror of blood! There were pools of it where he'd stood and sat, hand prints on walls and dressers where he'd braced himself. Blood pooled around his still body and made the thin gown stick to his slender frame.

We tried to wake him, but he was far beyond our childish ability to help or revive him. We didn't know what it was to be gay, or why it was bad, but we'd seen people die before. Uncle Benni was dying.

"The world!? The world don't give a damn about you. They wouldn't piss down your throat if your guts were on fire!"

It seems that two guys accosted him outside of a gay bar with large knives, thinking that intoxication and queer equaled soft, easy money. They call it 'rolling fags'. They were wrong. Benni still had a bloody bottle opener in his pocket and a blood-soaked wad of cash, two hundred and eighty some odd dollars. You see, he'd promised my sister and I that he'd take us to the carnival on the waterfront and didn't want to let us down.

He came home from the hospital with bandages everywhere and more than three hundred stitches. My grandmother had his brothers place him on a couch she'd made up for him in the living room. She walked him to the bath when he needed, changed his bandages, and took care of him like he was who he was – her child.

My other uncles were proud of him, and I noticed that their jokes included him after that. Things had changed. The rest of the family could see that there was more – a lot more – than being gay to the loved one lying on the couch all cut up. It's a shame he had to be cut open that bad for them to see what was inside, how special he was to us.

Victor 'Benni' Deloney would pass away in his sleep from pneumonia in a room full of family and friends, none of whom ever knew him. I got this time and never got the chance to say good-bye. I have no idea just where his spirit is today, but I promise that he's putting on one hell of a show.

I also have no idea why we, with all our flaws, sins and contradictions, are so quick to place conditions and labels on those we set out to love, as though who someone else is constitutes an attack on us. My glory and my sins are my own.

I don't think my uncle Benni was looking for agreement when he would stay away for so long, alone in the world. I remember the force of his smile on that couch. He loved his family who loved him back, at least on that day. No, I think he stayed away looking for *clan, kin, la familia.* He tramped home on that cold winter's night so he could die among his people because we were all he had. I was happy we could all be there for him. If not us, then who? I just hope we were enough, that he knew he was more than that for my sister and me.

This One Is For You

by Carter Cooper

Unfortunately, I've been incarcerated the majority of my adulthood, in and out of correctional facilities since the tender age of seventeen; more so in, rather than out. Although considered a late bloomer when compared to some of my felonious fellow men, none-the-less, here I am, an equally welcomed recidivist.

As a young man, the revolving 'ins and outs' never affected me, or apparently, I was too naive to realize the effects that were in fact taking place. So what if I lost my right to vote, own a gun or leave the country, I was a 'street n-bomb' and jail and prison were almost a certainty, sort of an occupational hazard that came with the lifestyle.

Never once did I realize the emotional and psychological toll the continual stints of confinement were taking. I've spent from two weeks in jail to thirteen years and nine months straight in prison, a total of five individual trips to prison, and I'm currently serving a 7-9 year sentence. Now I'm just learning the lesson I should've grasped decades ago.

The cumulative amount of time that I've spent chained, shackled, and caged surrounded by concrete and steel has completely desensitized me in regards to common human emotion. No, I'm not professing to be some deranged psychotic killer, but things that once meant something have lost tremendous, if not all, value to me.

Birthdays have become just another day, and holidays are the worst, most boring and slowest times of the year. I dread to see them, knowing the feelings they are bound to stir. "Bah-humbug'. These are only a fraction of the losses I've experienced.

I've lost friends and family who weren't mentally ready or mature enough to 'ride-a-bid' with me, but I understand now, that is an earnest request. The commitment and dedication required to stand by someone incarcerated can be emotionally taxing, not to mention someone who is repeatedly returning.

I've also lost family and friends to old age, ill health, accidents and the same 'street life' that has stolen so much of my very own life. None of this having any exceeding affect, all just casualties along the way.

During one of my short stints home, 'on the streets', 'free', I managed to create a child. But, just like every other time, Daddy was hell bent on returning to the pen.

While in the county jail, with the mother of my child alone, needy and months into her pregnancy, I pledged to my mother all the things I planned to do right if only God gave me a chance. I swore to do right by my little girl.

Now, let me preface this next part by saying, I'm a bonafide 'mama's boy' and proud of it. There's nothing I love more than my mother and nothing I wouldn't do for her, but I just couldn't seem to 'keep my behind' out of prison.

While proclaiming my new found inspiration and reason for doing things the right way – my daughter – my mom said, "Well, son, why can't you just do it for yourself? I understand you doing it for your daughter, but you need to do it for yourself... Stay free for yourself... Love yourself."

The words struck a chord, not simply resonating, but finding root in my mind, heart, and spirit. It was only months later when I faced my greatest fear – I lost my mother while incarcerated. I received the news while in the 'hole' and on my father's birthday. Adding insult to injury, I wasn't allowed to attend the funeral nor any closed viewing. Never given the chance to say, "goodbye", or "I love you", or "I'm sorry."

No matter how callous I've become through the years of confinement, this pain managed to penetrate my core, my soul, my very being.

Where do I now draw my inspiration to endure my hardship of incarceration? From my daughter, my mother and her words, "Do it for yourself, son."

"For I consider that the sufferings of this present time are not worth comparing with the glory that is going to be revealed to us." - Romans 8:18

Tommy

by John Green

I knew Tommy for over 20 years. He was a friend
– not as close as some, closer than others. He was
usually upbeat, always working and often watching
and betting on sports – mostly football. Like
myself, he loved the Rockets, Texans and Astros.
His only flaw, from my viewpoint, was that when
they were losing, he lost faith in his teams. Maybe
it was because he always bet his heart and not his
head, causing him to take some losses, but we'd
always laughed about it later.

I'd see him walking to work in the hallway and I'd call out, "Tommy!"

He'd answer, "How are you, John?" When he asked how I was, I knew he was sincere – not just talking or going through the motions. He really cared.

I think Tommy was a good guy who got caught up in the moment. Whatever he did to get himself here, I never asked because whatever it was, it was long ago, and the person that did it didn't exist anymore.

Tommy died of a sudden heart attack last night. I don't know his exact age, probably something close to mine. What I do know is – I'm one friend short.

Rest in peace, brother.

The Freest Spirit

by Terry Robinson

Dear Bear,

Writing this letter is harder than I thought, but for you – it is worth trying. I've never known anyone to write a dog before. Maybe that's because no dog has ever meant so much to someone. It's crazy to think where we both ended up – you buried somewhere in an unmarked grave and me worse off than dead. That's what Death Row is, Bear – a place between life and death. It's where people are deliberately kept alive long enough to anguish over the fear of being executed, tormented until all peace of mind is used up. Only then are we ripe for slaughter. How I got here on Death Row is too long a story and too depressing for the details – but, do you remember the guy next door whom I was cool with? ...turns out he wasn't so cool. I may never know why, but he accused me of taking another man's life during a robbery. Can you believe that? That's why I couldn't get home.

Anyway, getting back to the purpose of this letter. Bear, I had a dream about you just now. Hold on! Before you start bouncing around with those lofty cartwheels of yours, you should know it wasn't a good dream. In fact, it was probably the saddest thing I've ever dreamt, even though part of me wishes I could've stayed under. I woke feeling unfulfilled, like when waiting your whole life for something to happen, then realizing five seconds too late that it's gone. But I believe the dream was necessary, it put things in perspective. I now realize that in life, I left a lot of people behind.

So, the dream – it started out with me finally being released from Death Row. I was given some clothes and a severance package, but when I got outside, no one was at the gate. No family. No friends. No news cameras covering the story. It was as though any relevance I had owned had succumbed to my absence, and the world had moved on without me. I headed home, but when I got there, it wasn't the same house I remembered. The place was trashy and run-down with neglect, nothing left of the garden but wilted stems. The barn where we held so many of our family outings was now a crumbling derelict, trying to weather the times. All the holiday memories we made in that barn, and now it was no more than a safety hazard. Then I noticed a strange-looking structure. It looked like an igloo made of wood. And who do I see hobbling out from this dog house... yep. Bear – *it was you*.

You looked so mangy, worn-out and pitiful. Your eyes drooped with the age of years past. You looked like a dog that had been to hell and back with one foot still on the other side. The chain around your neck whined and creaked with the rust of twenty years. Your semblance, I hardly recognized. Then you looked at me and wagged your tail, and something in it spoke of you. I wouldn't have guessed that any feeling could amount to walking off Death Row after twenty years, but seeing you was an unspeakable joy. And to think you'd waited for me all that time. The gratefulness brought me to my knees. You then bound into my arms with your incessant tongue laps and tail thrashing. No homecoming reception was ever more welcoming.

I was struck with the fact that you had been tethered on a chain for more than two decades. Blame set in on me like a scolding tongue for my leaving you to suffer so. Then I remembered... we never kept you on a chain. My eyes stung with the indecency. It seemed you were also unjustly serving time. I stormed off towards the house, ready to spit fire at the new tenants and demand the key to let my dog loose, but when I burst through the door, spraying glass shards and splinters, I unintentionally shattered the dream.

There is no ache like waking up to the longing of a friend who has never let me down. I kept trying to get back to sleep to rescue you and discovered that the most meaningful things in life are the most elusive. So, you see – it wasn't a good dream at all, except for the joy of seeing you again. It made me realize what my sudden absence must've been like for you, how you must've felt abandoned by me.

Did you know the first time I saw you waiting inside the fence, I was reluctant and afraid. I was just dropped off by a parole officer, fresh out of prison that day. I wasn't aware we even had a dog. I guess my fears stemmed from learning of the era when White supremacists set upon Black people with their dogs. I mistook your panting, pouncing, and acting so unafraid of me as a clear sign of your aggression. But then you settled down and let me pet you, and I realized that all you wanted to do was play. My first impression of you was so unfair. Maybe that is the real source of my guilt.

Needless to say, I was wrong about you, Bear. You just didn't have it in you to hurt anyone. Well – there was that time when you snagged ahold the pants of that sheriff, but hell, you were only trying to get him off top of me. I remember thinking, *'this crazy dog gonna get hisself killed'*. Nobody had ever risked their life for me like that. I was so freaking proud of you.

I guess I should talk a little more about whatever since this will probably be the last time. It's not really considered normal behavior for people to write to their deceased pets. I don't mind coming off as weird; that's just another word for unique, and sometimes it's the most abnormal approach that is the only path to closure.

Often enough, there are times when I felt that you were the only one I could talk to, when I could do without anyone's judgment or advice – I just needed somebody to listen. So many late nights I came home with my pockets heavy from all the dirt I'd done and my conscience weighing on my shoulders. I thought I had to wrong people to survive in the streets, when really I was just trying to be seen. My coming home to you was the only time when I felt normal. With you I could be my ugly self. I would unload all the day's baggage at the doorstep while you lay curled at my feet, listening as my silent resolve. Bear – I can't tell you how much having your ear meant to me. Hell, I've told you shit I ain't told no one else. And on those rare nights when I didn't drop by to unlatch your kennel and chat... well, on those nights my shame was a bit too heavy.

I'm sorry I couldn't make it back to you, Bear, in both the dream and reality. I just didn't know that my doing so much dirt would get other people's dirt on me. I know you waited for me, and that must've sucked – wondering why all the late night walks around the neighborhood ended without reason, why all our fun just stopped. I want you to know that it wasn't because I abandoned you, Bear – not intentionally. No. I didn't come back because I, myself, am tethered by a red jumpsuit and Death Row has a really short reach. I keep on seeing that chain around your neck. I hope that wherever you are – somebody there will take it off. If not, I don't know how the spirit world works, but I promise to take care of it when I get there.

So long, old friend, and thanks for all the times when your company gave me solace. There is no loyalty like a dog's love. And, yep... I learned that from you.

Always, your trusted friend and spirit brother,

Chanton

I Was Her Son

by Carter Cooper

I felt alone today, by myself in a great big world, my mind and heart yearning for a familiar closeness that just wasn't there.

I guess for the first time I faced the gravity of my reality. I am, in fact, alone, by myself, detached from the world at large – a barren island of sorts, surrounded by a sea of destitution and braving a storm of bereavement... all alone.

As do most, I too took for granted having a place of refuge amid adversity, finding truth in that bitter sentiment – *'you don't know what you've got until its gone'*.

At one point in time, no matter where or what I faced, there was a place I could find solace and security, a harmonic vibration, a channel I could tune in that reassured comfort, confidence and completeness. It was a source of strength that superseded all anxiety, fortified fortitude and boosted morale.

My quiet place silenced the chaotic chatter, providing a sense of still, and the much needed presence of peace. A stronghold, shielding against every advancement of the adversary, the cornerstone of an unwavering foundation.

Loving arms, listening ears, and a well of wisdom that shone like a beacon of light; giving guidance along my journey. If I veered off course or found myself lost and astray, that same light beckoned, correcting any misdirection. It was a luminous love that calmed every raging water, gently guiding me home.

No matter the distance, if I called, she'd come. Despite the odds, she stood tall, head high and proud... that I was her son. My mothership has sailed, leaving me behind... alone... by myself... another prisoner of time.

Isn't Nearly Fifty Years Of Punishment Enough For Leonard Bradford-Bey?

by Ricardo Ferrell

Growing up in Detroit on Brady & Hastings in a once vibrant and bustling neighborhood where blacks owned several businesses and created jobs and livelihoods for many who resided there, Leonard aka Leanbone – a nickname given to him by his uncle due to his skinny frame – learned early on how to survive by adapting and finding ways to cope with the many challenges he faced. It was during those years, he experienced his own personal trauma as well as witnessing police brutality. Those experiences led him down a road of dysfunction, despair and destruction. Leonard shared with me how his nearly fifty year incarceration has taken its toll on his health. He now battles cancer, requires a cane in order to get around and has a prisoner assistant him with his meals and other necessities.

Leonard attributes the path he chose in good part to bad choices and poor decision-making, which led him to a life of crime that ultimately resulted in a man losing his life during a stick-up attempt. Leonard expresses regret and remorse for the harm he caused the victim, their family, his family, the black community and society as a whole because that's who was impacted by his reckless and out-of-control behavior.

This writer can relate to Leonard and the harm he caused because I am also responsible for a young black man losing his life to an act of senseless violence. It's sad that we didn't value the life of another human-being and acted so impulsively. However, men like Leonard Bradford-Bey, who is now almost seventy years old, realize the devastation of past criminal behavior. He strives relentlessly to deter the same behavior in younger men and has become a well-known mentor and example that others can follow despite being behind bars. Even so, as I peer into Leonard's eyes, I see agony and shame for past deeds. Leonard's health is rapidly deteriorating, and at this point, with the life expectancy of a black man, he is living on what we call 'borrowed time'. The stress of having to deal with cancer and not receiving adequate healthcare can lead to more health issues. I have been around Leonard for the past 35 years or more and watched him go from an athletically-inclined, able-bodied individual, to that of a nearly handicapped man in need of constant assistance to get around on a daily basis.

It saddens my heart and pulls at the core of my soul to see my friend become slowly debilitated before my eyes. If punishing offenders for crimes they've been convicted of includes this form of torturous madness, having them deal with life ending illnesses like cancer, heart disease, and kidney failure behind these bars – then I must ask... At what point is prolonged incarceration enough, especially if it has met the threshold of its intended penological purpose? In other words, if the punitive and retributive aspects have been reached, why not then focus on the rehabilitative and transformative aspects of an individual's growth and maturation out of criminality? Leonard has evolved and worked for his transformation, even earning a one year certificate towards his Associates Degree.

Over the last four decades, I've had to witness countless folks like Leonard suffer and wither away to near nothingness. The reality of it hits home because I can honestly put myself in Leonard's shoes as I am approaching the same age bracket and have serious health concerns as well. I realize that many of us have committed terrible acts of violence, and people have lost their lives. However many of us, like Leonard, have shown and genuinely expressed our remorse and sorrow, shown sincere empathy, and taken full responsibility for our actions which led up to the crime and the offense itself.

In the early '80s I was housed at Marquette Branch Prison, an old prison known for its vicious and volatile violence and stark similarities and resemblance to Alcatraz because it sits less than 50 yards off Lake Superior. One day a prisoner was aggressively harassing a young female prison guard who was terrified. Leonard happened to walk up and see the fear in the guard's eyes and the danger she was in. He immediately intervened and saved her from harm. He didn't consider the harm he was putting himself in, but that was Bradford-Bey for you. He wasn't little Leanbone anymore, he was 6 foot tall and 260 lbs. – Grandman. He transitioned from being known as

Leanbone to Grandman because he became a
political activist and spiritual leader. He was a
straight up cat, who didn't particularly like to see
anyone taken advantage of. I believe in my heart
that if Leonard was to be released tomorrow, he
could contribute something good to his
community. If you were to talk with anyone here
in the Michigan Prison System, I have no doubt
whatsoever they would agree with me that he is the
last of the Mohicans and surely a soul worth saving
from this madness of prolonged unnecessary
incarceration and the physical and mental
suffering he deals with everyday. I pray the day
comes they release Leonard and let him live the
remaining days of his life on the other side of the
gate.

*Dedicated to Leonard 'Grandman' Bradford-Bey
– From One Soul Brother to Another.*

[Editor's Note: Since the original writing,
Leonard lost his fight to live.]

A Real Soul Brother

It only happens every millennium that you meet someone with a soul like our beloved Leonard "Grandman" Bradford-Bey.

So, in remembrance of you, Leanbone, I want you to know your soul has touched those of us who were close to you. Remember back in the day when you were growing up on Brady near Hastings? Back then you were a young cat that stood out amongst the rest. Even then you were destined to impact the lives of the people you encountered.

Although your physical form has passed from this earth - your soul remains and the conscious ones who are still here will always be in tune with your spirit.

May your soul rest for an eternity and the words of wisdom you imparted help the multitude and uplift a fallen humanity for generations to come. I am going to miss you Leanbone, but always know you'll be here forever.

Peace & Love,

Your Soul Brother,

Ricardo

Happy Holidays

Holidays and traditions from prison are often a double-edged sword, with prisons serving marginally better meals and those living there wanting to hold dear lifelong traditions while struggling with the grief of *not* being 'home' for the holidays.

This Christmas –
Imagining Something
Different,

by Ricardo Ferrell

Growing up, it seemed every Christmas my imagination would expand more than the year before. I would hope for everything I ever wanted, but in reality my hopes were diminished. At times I only got the Goodfellow's box and a few other items underneath the Christmas tree. It was tight for us back then, the only means of income in our household, like many others, was the public assistance check known as ADC or Welfare every two weeks. Man, those were some embarrassing times as a youngster. I would go to some of my friends' houses and see all kinds of toys in their front rooms under huge trees. I don't think my young heart could form any envy toward them because most all my friends would share their many toys with me. They'd let me ride their new bikes, and play with their electric trains, race car sets, and even their Rockem Sockem Robots.

Although we didn't have much in the form of material riches, we had a kind of wealth in our hearts which was demonstrated by the love and appreciation we had for each other. I recall my mother and I decorating our tree with Christmas lights, an assortment of bulbs, candy canes, artificial icicles, and ornaments to make our tree look its very best. I was happy to crawl under everyday and pour water into the stand to keep it fresh. We usually waited until Christmas Eve to go down to the Eastern Market and buy us a tree because the price would drop to only a dollar or two. It was an exciting time during the holiday season, and I enjoyed helping to select our tree every year.

On Christmas we would enjoy my mother's deliciously cooked meal before heading over to visit with relatives, and I could always expect several Christmas presents waiting for me at my Aunt Mae's house. She was what you call hood rich and lived ghetto fabulous. Her house was laid out with the best furniture from Margolis, an expensive furniture outlet where she bought mostly all Italian-style layouts. She was never stingy with her money or riches, and gladly gave us whatever we needed. So, we might have been borderline living way below the poverty level at our household, but it was a completely different story when I went over to my auntie's house. My Christmas changed dramatically and so did my attitude of not having much because at my aunt's house on Seyburn in West Village, I had everything I wanted. That is how I could imagine something different every Christmas morning back when I was growing up, and even though I might be confined behind bars, I can still experience those same fond memories at Christmas time.

While the meals in here can't compare to the ones my mother and Aunt Mae cooked, where the collard greens, sweet potatoes, baked turkey, deep fried chicken, chitlins, baked ham, potato salad, string beans, cranberry sauce, and butter milk cornbread would literally melt in your mouth, not to mention the best banana pudding you could ever taste, I'm still appreciative because there's millions upon millions of people who go hungry every single day, many starving to death. I have no room to complain about a poorly prepared and cooked prison holiday meal. What I normally do is close my eyes and imagine those delicious meals I used to eat at a real dinner table. Believe it or not, a smile always comes across my face because I can still imagine tasting what I miss so much.

Today is Thanksgiving, and we're on 'quarantine status' for at least fourteen days as a result of

nearly 200 of us in this housing unit testing
positive for COVID, which means we've been
eating cold, poorly prepared meals three times a
day out of styrofoam trays since this past Monday.
The holiday meal of processed turkey, dressing,
mash potatoes and gravy will be served the same
way later, and the same meal will be served on
Christmas Day, but I'll do as I've done for nearly
forty years in here, close my eyes and imagine
something different.

Happy Elation Day Falls on December 29!

By Joshua Kenyon

Holidays are often lost on the incarcerated, memories of a time lost that many may never find again. Often, I find myself saddened by a cheerful Christmas spirit, or thoughts of a Thanksgiving feast, sad because right now I can only pretend that not being with loved ones and family doesn't hurt, knowing they are missing me too.

Yet, I find myself celebrating a more unorthodox day, my own little holiday. It may be meaningless to most, but it means the world to me. I have found a day I will always celebrate, a day I can smile for, a day that I take stock of all that I am grateful for. On that day, I always eat a big meal of whatever I can scrounge out of my box, all with great joy and happiness.

What is this day I find solace in? To that I say — what comes after a sentence? For many of us, the correct answer is appeals. My special day of celebration is connected to my appeals. It is a day that gave me another chance at life. I won my 35(c) Ineffective Assistance of Counsel and my Rule 33 Motion For A New Trial on December 29, 2017. This is my Christmas, my New Year, all my holidays rolled into one.

I won't poison my celebration with all the legalities, the 'should haves', 'what ifs' and everything else that I might not still agree with. I don't want to take away from or diminish my special holiday in any way. All that matters to me is that on December 29, 2017, my 198 year prison sentence had the door opened, and I was given a chance at life again. Turning 198 years into twenty is something worth celebrating, let me tell you.

Due to my newly found personal holiday, maybe the orthodox holidays will some day feel special again. Maybe one day I will be 'that guy' with the annoying overly cheerful Christmas spirit, or have a Thanksgiving feast, and maybe some day somebody will make me their Valentine. One day, I'll be able to draw designs in the air with sparklers and hide Easter eggs in the neighborhood.

One day, I'll be able to do all of that, but for me, my favorite holiday will always be Elation Day, December 29.

A Christmas Card From One Prison To Another

by Delaine Jones

Charles,

Hey, I'm not sure how much love you get through the mail, brah, so I thought I'd push some your way. It's free, so why on earth wouldn't I give it away? You only have to pay for it, if you refuse to pass it on. Funny the truths that you'll trip over in these little cages, right?

My name is DeLaine Jones, and I've been on lockdown for the last thirty-three years. I'm also a writer for WITS. I've been reading about you for awhile now, meaning to get at you, but only now making the time. I'm not sure if you've read any of my work, but I'd like to write a piece to you.

I'm not looking to gain from the war you're fighting to take your next breath. But I don't just look like this, I'm really black! I speak, read, watch and write through these bars, into and about a struggle that I can't physically take part in. But even as I gasp and choke my way to hope... I see you, brah!

Back in the dayz when we were in chains on the other side of these bars, we as black people used to speak to other black people whom we had never met. Not simply as a courtesy, but from a genuine concern, a want to help someone who's chains, pains and scars resembled our own. I personally believe that if I can in any small way, shape, or fashion, help you be heard – it is *the reason* for my 'hood card'. As I started out, you've got to give it away to keep it coming in, brah.

I'm serving ninety years for crimes I committed when I was seventeen years old. Though I don't have a date to die, I too know the value of hope, how being touched can alter the quality of the air you breath. That at times it's easier to let go rather than fight to hold on for another day. That at times, we need to be held on to. Today, I've got ya, brah!

So, this is us passing on an old dirt road in the deep South... *"What's up blood, you good?"* – meaning, if you need me so you can hide for a awhile and rest till you are able to run again – I've got you. I've got a scrap or two of food that'll tide you over too! *"You good, cuzz-in?"*

I've only ever written about my life and the people who've passed through it. It's crazy how I can hear their voices at times when I write. Has that ever happened to you? For me, it comes when people encourage me. It's then that I hear my granny say,

"We are all that we've got." Only the encouragement comes from some place other than my blood. So I expect the givers of those words to give up at some point, to wake up tomorrow and they too will have 'passed through.'

No family, I'm not in the same part of the river, but I can see you being drowned from where I'm being held down. Those words are needed, welcomed even, but as we both know this is *way* too much water for either of us to be tryin' to drink!

People will try to rob you of your anger, telling you to be *'be calm'*. But as a black man in the system, *'be calm'* is code for *'stop struggling so that I can kill you!'*

Charles, I'm not sure if I've ever met an innocent man before. But I do know that they hand out far too many of these sentences without revealing every bit of information that they can get their hands on, laying it out for all to see, rather than allowing the D.A. to decide what it suits his case to present. Who knows a diamond's worth until it's seen? Under magnification at that!

It's the systemic contradictions and racist collusions that gall. To be willing to seek a mans' life as payment for a life – but to be negligent in that you don't turn over *every single stone* in your quest, this in respect of the very priceless substance you claim to hold so dear.

Life!

Charles, I call the collusion systemic and racist because it's not an accident that you're black nor how you've come to be on death row. Your legal counsel never bothered to ask basic and obvious questions that would have led to the truth. How does anyone who's passed the bar in this country allow testimony about a sexual assault without the challenge of a rape kit? Evidence? Examination? Something!

Your counsel stood by and let that become part of what the jury heard and a *fact*, agreed to but not supported by evidence. The D.A. knew it and your counsel had to *know* it. But it gets better!

The medical examiner shows up *without* the physical evidence he gathered! Doesn't even mention it. The D.A. shows up *without* the only physical evidence that can suggest that you didn't, in fact, commit the crime. The Judge allows it all to happen, and your counsel, none of the sworn officers of the Court, think that it is noteworthy? Each of their perspectives center on the same physical evidence, which happens to have been collected in a rape kit, and none of them bother to produce the only existing physical evidence? And we 'the public' are to simply ignore the obviously choreographed farce?! Allow you to kill a man based on the above?!

A lone woman from Virginia went to Texas and found the rape kit twenty years later. It was never lost.

Charles, I have no idea at what temperature the naiveté of white people is burned away. Many

seem baffled as to why black men would be so
desperate to escape the *mere presence* of police if
they were not guilty – as if guilt justifies murder.

For some, it's the walk on the sun that has fried
the brain's ability to believe what it's seeing, a
quick flicker of a thing that is banished in a single
blink of the eye. In that glint, they reach for
justification that makes them okay with
themselves and cools their soul. They can then
dismiss and pardon and excuse themselves.

In that flicker, they find themselves on an old dirt
road in the deep South, passing a person who's
breathing hard from running. They see the pain of
the other's soul reflected in eyes they quickly turn
away from, denying them to be like their own.
They don't offer the other a place to rest until they
can run again, a scrap of food to tide them over.
"You good, bro?" only crosses their minds.

In that encounter they find themselves face to face
with themselves. Their guilt isn't about Jim Crow
or slavery or things of the past, but what happened

this morning. The modern-day lynching of a black man that took place in a courtroom in Texas. But hold tight, brah! Charles, be encouraged! *If you need me so you can hide for a while and rest till you are able to run again – I've got you. I've got a scrap or two of food that'll tide you over too!*

Collateral Damage

Jamycheal Mitchell inspired WITS. The non-profit nor this book would exist in their current form without his story. There were other factors, but his impact shaped *this*.

Jamycheal was a young man of 24 when he was found dead in a jail cell. He was jailed for stealing a soda, a candy bar and a snack cake from a convenience store in Virginia. Upon arrival at the jail, he weighed 182 pounds. Upon his death about 100 days later, he weighed 144 pounds. A young man with a history of mental illness was locked up for stealing food, and how he existed and died, surrounded by urine and feces, under the care of Virginia's Hampton Roads Regional Jail for the next few months sparked WITS. There are countless more 'Jamycheals' across the country – 'collateral damage'.

Although Jamycheal's story and his death are the foundation for WITS, after working with writers for several years, I came to realize some of them were actually innocent, and some of those innocent lived on death row. I shared my concern with an attorney friend, and she tried to put it into perspective. People want to have roads, she said. People die on roads. Society accepts those deaths, the 'collateral damage', because they are willing to

take an acceptable amount of loss for the greater
good of having roads.

Yet... we continually try to make vehicles and
roads safer – why not the justice system? Or is it
because the collateral damage within mass
incarceration is acceptable, for the most part
impacting a *specific* segment of society?

I Am Often Asked

by Terry Robinson

"What does it feel like to be innocent on Death Row?"

My answer?

"A setback for mankind."

I was born in the '70s to black parents in black times in a world that was gray at best. My earliest lessons on guilt were not determined by wrongdoings, but by the color of one's skin. I saw the guilty as they were dipped in tar and strung up for public viewing, or set upon for sitting down to eat. Guilt then becomes a psychological impression on the minds of black communities; a sense of guilt that is the origin of the criminal mind – a reflection of how we feel. Guilt is the cultural identity that leaves behind a trail of regrets, so I am dissociated with feeling innocent in a country that charges people guilty for having black skin.

I was convicted of the murder of a restaurant manager in April, 2000, and sentenced to die by a consenting jury by way of lethal injection. Arriving on Death Row, I conceded two things – my innocence was insignificant and justice grotesquely one-sided. I decided that neither guilt nor innocence had brought me there – it was powerlessness. I was powerless to take charge of my life and break the cycle of recidivism. I was put on the path to prison at the age of seven, the time I first stole, my impropriety promising to progress over time. By the age of twenty-seven, I was the product of circumstances and my road ended here, yet despite all my wrongdoings, still I did not deserve to be on Death Row.

I avoided eye contact with men, sparse with my words, afraid that my difference would show and the rapists, brutes and murderers would figure out I was not. There was no introduction guide to Death Row, but if there was, I imagined it would've read,

Innocence does not thrive here,

your hope is your despair.

For the first year, I uttered not a word about innocence, though the subject was one of recurrence, casually hinted at by some in conversations, while others were more straightforward. I wondered if my own innocence sounded as disingenuous as theirs when spoken aloud. The improbability of their innocence caused me to dismiss their claims as prison colloquialism.

Over time, I learned to shelve my innocence while emulating the hardened killers. I was wary and distrusting, argumentative, and constantly on the lookout for a fight. At night, sometimes, my mind broke free, much to my dismay. I never knew fantasizing could hurt so bad. I envisioned life as a working-class citizen, doing stringent work that was wearisome but decent, with a pension as opposed to a penalty. Other times, I grasped at the wilting memories of family and friends as their influence crumbled under their hefty absence, and their faces yielded to time.

Then came the biggest news... a Death Row man was freed from here after being awarded a new trial. I was skeptical, challenged his innocence, as he was someone I previously dismissed. Still the question lingered... what if he was innocent? And what if there were others? These men I'd subjected to my silent criticism, fostered by widespread belief. Unable to relate due to their menacing aura, my innocence was too fragile to trust, so I rejected them based solely on my preconceived notion. It was the very same rejection I feared. I wanted to be happy for a guy whose stay on Death Row was at its end, but with my errant dismissal of him and my own self interest, I was too ashamed.

As the years rolled by, cases were amended and death sentences overturned – mental retardation and the prohibiting of minors were enactments that saved lives. In some few cases, the men were exonerated on the likelihood of innocence, an unsettling error revealing that behind the virtue of our courts was depravity. There was a time when I presumed our judicial system stood on the right side of public service, but with the growing number of death sentences vacated, an alarming truth emerged. Wrongful convictions were not the result of legal mishaps – but a setback in the evolution of justice. It was a systemic trade-off, conviction rates in return for support at the ballots. On the verge of understanding how my injustice came to be, I was nowhere close to help, as I struggled to wish well those men who departed… their hope was my despair.

Every day I longed for my freedom until all my hope was spent, and I was left with nothing more than a stale existence. With each reversal, I felt sorely abandoned by the securities of the laws. I pondered the plausibility of my injustice and came away rejecting myself. I used recreational drugs, obscenities and conflict to propel my downward spiral. I severed outside connections, quit my aspirations and rigorously questioned my faith. It seemed my road didn't stop on Death Row, but I was headed to a place much darker, and no matter how far my mind drifted from my mad reality, the executions pulled me back.

On those nights I ached helplessly as the clock wound down on the lives of men tethered to a gurney. I wondered if they winced at the needle's prick like I did as a kid at the clinic, or closed their eyes in defiance to die alone. Done with feeling helpless, I put their deaths out of my mind and tried to remain unaffected by the executions until a death date arrived for a friend of mine… and my helplessness turned to surrender.

It was thirteen years later before I gained some clarity into the disorder taking place in my life. It began with written essays that chronicled my past offenses, offenses unrelated to my stay here, restoring in me a sense of worth. Accountability for my previous wrongs – saved my life. Without it, I would've given up. With the many death sentences being vacated, I couldn't wait one more turn, and through accountability, I discovered there was redemption behind these walls, the potential to reinvent the principles of humanity – and the most promising yet was the willingness of these men to die with more dignity than that with which they lived.

So, what is it like to be innocent on Death Row is best answered by the word 'unrest'. It is a constant grinding of the mind in an effort to determine how we tolerate such criminal indecency. My being wrongfully convicted is a laborious affliction under the stigmatic strain of disbelief – a strain that offered one resolve for me, complacency for my accusers. It's lonely being innocent with no one to talk to about the certainty of my innocence. And frightening. Only Ichabod Crane, a character from my childhood, terrified me so. Often enough, being innocent feels pointless after 21 years of punishment, when death is no longer a menacing possibility but a welcome alternative.

Being innocent on Death Row is soulfully depressing, granting little peace of mind. It is my fight to hold on to the hope I deserve, when the culpability isn't mine to bear. My innocence is no more relevant than the next man's guilt when the ink on our status reads the same – and yet, what does it matter, guilt or innocence, in a nation such as our own, where both are punishable by death.

Surviving The Day!

by Charles Mamou, Jr.

I've been on Texas death row since November 1999, and was first held with the others at the 'old death row housing', Ellis One Unit, that provided group recreation, church services, work programs – camaraderie. There was a different vibe then. Sure, men were still being led like sheep to the slaughter in record numbers, and sure, a few were innocent, some wrongly convicted and many guilty, but the deprivation of social and human interaction in all forms was not as glaring then because we were allowed to play four-on-four basketball games outdoors, able to share hugs with one another, able to lean on one another when one had some bad news and needed a shoulder to cry on, and we were able to pray in groups. Some sat around tables playing card games, chess, or just sat in silence watching a movie or sports on ESPN. In no way am I exulting that existence, because I can never be content as long as I am being held in chains. I'm innocent. But the reality of living at Ellis during that time was 'doable'. Man was not alone.

March 2000, everything changed, including death row's location and current housing. From the moment we arrived on Polunsky Unit we were handcuffed and chained, from our ankles to our stomach to our hands by one long chain and ordered off the heavily armed buses and stripped nude for the whole world to see. That became the moment I knew everything was different.

We were placed in single man cells on sections that held fourteen cells per each of the six sections that encased one of six pods. Gone were work programs, group recreation, church services and all forms of physical contact that we once enjoyed. Morale was so low, it could be sensed within the thickness of the silence. Suicides and suicide attempts spiked that first year. A black, middle-aged inmate from Dallas, Clark, started shouting madly, daily, as if he was Paul Revere, saying things like, "In five years this place will be a place of madness!" Many laughed, thinking him already mad.

Clark and three others would die within the first five-hundred days, from unknown natural causes. They simply dropped dead in their cells. Men as young as 26 and as old as 51 were now remembered as 'how did they die'. Though many surmised their depressive stress became too much to bear.

As time passed, men started self-mutilating, one cutting his penis off and throwing it out of his cell.

Another, so consumed with religious material, set himself on fire. One man stabbed himself in the jugular and made not a sound. Before he bled out, he wrote, 'I'm innocent', in his own blood on the wall. The following day, the Courts granted him a stay to look into his claims, to no avail. One man ate his own eye, then ate the other. He said it tasted like chicken. Many hung themselves. A few started eating their own feces. An overwhelming number sought help from the mental health department which provided them with experimental psychiatric drugs that kept them in a nebulous, zombie-like state, in which they slept all day and could not function in a coherent manner. Inmate-friends at Ellis became inmate-enemies on Polunsky. Staff and inmate assaults rose substantially. The ugly reality the aftermath, when loneliness became dictator.

Clark's prophetic words soon became a beacon to the fact that man crumbles from the starvation of physical interaction.

I'm not exempt from suicidal thoughts, the cancer known as depression swallowing me whole from time-to-time, more often than I care to dwell on. At times I'm consumed with thoughts of dying, being murdered, never getting free again and never getting another chance to feel the warm lips of a lover. Will I ever again salivate over the seasonings and texture of a home cooked meal from my mother? Who says insanity is all that bad? My mind does play tricks on me.

I want to be free. My freedom was molested from me with false allegations, and I struggle every moment to exist within these solitary confines, my survival not based on my courage or strength, but on those who write to me, encourage me and love me unconditionally. I survive for them.

I do not know what tomorrow will bring. I'm out of appeals and the only step left is to get an execution date. That notion weighs heavily on me, but I have given my friends a promise to continue to be me until my soul is liberated from the manacles of my flesh.

Know this – I love you. Doesn't matter if you hate me or support me. None of it matters. For without love, we all cease to survive the day.

Entries From My Journal

entries from the journal of Terry Robinson

Note. These entries are a small attempt to touch on the surface of what it is like to be innocent and on death row. How did Terry Robinson end up on death row? Two people physically connected to the crime scene accused Robinson of murder, saying he confessed to them. That's it. These entries are not edited, but shared in their original format.

February 5, 2014 (Wednesday, 12:43 a.m.)

Sitting here on my bed staring off into nothingness as so many thoughts fill my head about where I am and why I am here. Does it even matter whether I'm innocent or not? Am I destined to die here regardless? Sometimes I wish they would just get it over with. The heartache and pain from missing my family is unbearable – death has to be better than this. Then I think... does this make me suicidal to prefer death over agony? To know sadness day in and day out for more than fifteen years is a recipe for insanity. Constantly engulfed in darkness. Always alone, even when others are present. Avoiding my reflection in the mirror each morning as I am afraid to face myself and the reality that is my life, or so my death. I may never get to hug my mother again or go fishing with my father. To many others that knew me, I am long forgotten; a conviction and a sentence has erased me from existence in all the ways that count. The tears are more frequent and the numbness is without end. Some say, 'prayer changes things'. If that's true, then the only thing it seems to have changed in my mind is that prayer changes things.

My hope is not just fleeting – it has long fled, but who the hell cares?

July 9, 2014 (Wednesday, 1:05 p.m.)

Aw, man – I just got to meet Mr. Eugene Brown. What an experience. I've talked about the movie, *'Life Of A King'*, so much, and now I've met the man that inspired the movie. I was really surprised by his aura of normality – I was expecting much different. Now I realize it was his normalcy that gave such realness to his words. Dude is truly a powerful man, and I think his philosophy can potentially change the world. I am a King, and I do control the pieces of my life... definitely. I've gotta start making better decisions for myself if I want to finish with a strong and relevant end game. It was cool that Mr. Brown came out to see us – I'll carry the things he said to us forever. A true blessing to have experienced that today. I wish I could talk to my brother right now, I would pay it forward. We are all our own Kings. Wow – what a day.

September 2, 2014 (Tuesday, 7:46 pm)

Man, what a wonderful day – not necessarily for
me and especially not for all hating-ass envious
dudes who don't wanna see nobody get ahead, but
for Big Hen and the McCollum family. Dude went
home today – wow, man, how great is that. I was
speechless when I saw the news, but happy
nonetheless. I guess it does pay to have hope. I lost
my hope a long time ago and didn't even know it. I
held on for as long as I could, then I just stopped
believing in justice. I've gotta get my hope back –
sometimes things do get better.

My man, Big Hen. Good luck out there bruh, and
I'm gonna miss you.

February 3, 2015 (Tuesday, 11:14 pm)

I'm praying, God. I heard it said that you know
our hearts. Don't do me like everybody else has
done.

I Didn't Kill Mary

by Charles Mamou, Jr.

Since I've been on Texas' Death Row, where reading is the only natural form of entertainment, I have read a lot of history books. When I think of my situation, there is little difference between 1898 and 1998 – I was just a young, dumb, poor black kid who stood alone. I wasn't the first, and I wasn't the last. It was the norm. Racist and overzealous prosecutors saw me and those that look like me the same, 'a menace to society', deplorable and judicially dispensable, while off-colored jokes were made in the locker room, no one having the gumption to tell them in public.

Here's what I want people to know. Even after I was convicted and sentenced to die by a jury that looked nothing like me, I still blew it off. *'I'll win on appeal, 'cause there is no way I won't get action'.* I didn't know an appeal is just a maze of malleable interpretations of laws, many not even heard on appeal, getting 'procedurally barred'. The system only works if you have the money to move it in your favor.

I knew one thing in 1998. I didn't bring Mary to that night. I didn't kidnap Mary. I didn't kill Mary. And I sure as hell didn't rape her. My lawyers didn't care about me at all, told me that in five years I would win my case on appeal. I believed what I was told. Then five turned to ten and ten to twenty, and I realized America wasn't about the truth. The D.A. had evidence during trial that their own witness' were lying – but said nothing. They had phone records that show phone calls were being made all night, but both witnesses claimed they were asleep.

I'm not the first man to sit innocent on Death Row. I know the real meaning of HATE and what it feels and tastes like to be hated. The difference between me and them – I don't hide from who I was and who I am. And in case anyone wants to know – you're damn right, I'm mad.